The son of a prosperous Dublin solicitor, John was educated at Rugby School and Balliol, theological college, he became a writer. His George Bernard Shaw – was published to wide acclaim. Unable to repeat this success, he spent the pre-war years living in poverty. His fortunes changed in 1940 when he became a farm labourer working on the land in Dorset and Sussex. These experiences were published as the classic *The Worm Forgives the Plough*.

In 1947, Collis' talents were officially recognized when he won the Heinemann Foundation Award for Literature.

He wrote biographies of Christopher Columbus, Havelock Ellis and Leo Tolstoy and is also celebrated for his works on natural phenomena in which he took a scientific subject and described it from the layperson's point of view. Full of curiosity for the things most of us take for granted, these are the works of which Collis was most proud.

BY THE SAME AUTHOR
ALL PUBLISHED BY HOUSE OF STRATUS

AN ARTIST OF LIFE: HAVELOCK ELLIS
BOUND UPON A COURSE
THE CARLYLES
CHRISTOPHER COLUMBUS
FAREWELL TO ARGUMENT
LEO TOLSTOY
LIVING WITH A STRANGER
MARRIAGE AND GENIUS
SHAW
THE SOUNDING CATARACT
THE VISION OF GLORY
THE WORM FORGIVES THE PLOUGH

An Irishman's England

JOHN STEWART COLLIS

First published in 1937
Copyright © John Stewart Collis

All rights reserved. No part of this publication may be reproduced, stored in a retrieval system, or transmitted, in any form, or by any means (electronic, mechanical, photocopying, recording, or otherwise), without the prior permission of the publisher. Any person who does any unauthorised act in relation to this publication may be liable to criminal prosecution and civil claims for damages.

The right of John Stewart Collis to be identified as the author of this work has been asserted.

This edition published in 2001 by House of Stratus, an imprint of
Stratus Holdings plc, 24c Old Burlington Street, London, W1X 1RL, UK.
Also at: Suite 210, 1270 Avenue of the Americas, New York, NY 10020, USA.

www.houseofstratus.com

Typeset, printed and bound by House of Stratus.

A catalogue record for this book is available from the British Library
and The Library of Congress.

ISBN 1-84232-639-2

This book is sold subject to the condition that it shall not be lent, resold, hired out, or otherwise circulated without the publisher's express prior consent in any form of binding, or cover, other than the original as herein published and without a similar condition being imposed on any subsequent purchaser, or bona fide possessor.

PREFACE

An Irishman educated in England can neither pose as a foreign observer nor pontificate as a detached outsider. But he has this advantage, that while having experienced England as thoroughly as an Englishman, he is able to record his impressions with an unEnglish bias.

I have divided the book into two parts. In the first I have attempted by a series of pictures to give some account of what has particularly struck me about London and about the country. The second part, while also approaching the subject from the particular and personal experience, is an attempted continuous reflection on the political, the social and the cultural scene.

If large tracts of the national life are left out altogether, that is because this book is not an objective treatise.

J S COLLIS

CONTENTS

PART ONE

1 IMPRESSIONS AND REFLECTIONS IN LONDON   1
Approaching London — quality of hidden beauty — underground — endurance of the people — a journey — ocean of drabness — docks — ethical bent of the people — the fair, the orators, Armistice Day, the drama of Monarchy — silence of the traffic — symbols of Order — elephants and fogs — the great library — the factory — Nature's triumph in Piccadilly

2 IMPRESSIONS AND REFLECTIONS IN THE COUNTRY   27
Outward from London — the desolate valley — the emerald isle — the Spirit of History — wandering in the English Twilight — Hardy and Wordsworth — the villages — the manor houses — an ideal proposal — within the gate — Nature's triumph on the great highway

PART TWO

3 A UNITED PEOPLE   47
A nation more than others — parliamentary government — progress through gradualism — traditional in form, revolutionary at heart — next move now due — the Hunger Marchers — the quarter from which violence can be expected — impressions of the General Strike — democracy in England — foreign policy — the British Empire and the British character

4 SOME OF THE PEOPLE AND THEIR CHARACTERISTICS 62
On New Cross Station platform — the class-hierarchy — my prejudices — the English working man versus the Irish — classes immediately above — the "little man" — the gentleman — the public schools both cause and effect — principles of the gentleman, some disadvantages in self-repression, superb advantages in public life — personal supremacy — not really a "type" — happy when in action — self-expression in sport versus American — profound conception of play — games not taken seriously as in other countries — the anomaly of blood-sports — the deceiving hare

5 ENGLAND AND CULTURE 87
A civilized but not cultured people — attitude towards education — the new barbarians — levelling down — self-betrayal of the intelligentsia — the English mind, sincere but not serious, no passion for the absolute, views instead of convictions — no passionate theatre, standard of excellence, religious spirit — ingredients of the excellent entertainment — love of puzzles — attitude of universities — of the literary élite — no support for bearers of purely cultural values — deep love of money — the Press — the "scoop" versus feeling — popular journalism and literature — the English poets problem — leave-taking

PART ONE

1

IMPRESSIONS AND REFLECTIONS IN LONDON

The extravagance and eccentricity of the English never fail to astonish the outsider. They appear to preserve their balance by passing from one extreme to the opposite extreme, from the intemperance of meat-eating to the intemperance of vegetarianism, from the passion for hunting and gaming animals to the passion for protecting animals. Their craze for motion and speed is equalled by their craze for checking motion and speed – thus no incongruity was felt when Sir Malcolm Campbell after having driven at 252 miles an hour was photographed distributing prizes to bus-drivers under the sign of Safety First. Above all, they balance their enormous appetite for the countryside by an enormous appetite for building towns.

It is this last fact which engages one's attention so continually in England. There is no lovelier countryside in the world. In spite of this there is no country which fits into its limited space so many large and uninspiring towns. To the astonished traveller it seems as if something sinister must have happened or is presumed to happen to anyone who remains on the soil. One meets few people off the main roads; often one can go for miles without meeting a soul – while many of the solitudes of this land are more solitary in primeval stillness than the waste place of the imagination. The people have fled from their countryside. They have fortified themselves in big towns. A stranger walking through the island and knowing its size finds it difficult to believe that there are over forty-seven million people in it – an incredible thought.

Until he comes to London. The moment we enter London, however, the amount of the population ceases to surprise. In their passion for overdoing things the English have turned a whole county into a town! They are still adding to it, though few of them now think that it is too small.

It is a privilege to be born outside London. (Londoners should realize that this is still possible.) For then one can enter it – for the first time, and at all times – as an onlooker.

One should enter by train. The railway is one of the successes of civilization – and never more so than when it carries the traveller into London. Not exactly on the earth, nor wholly in the air, but in a half-earthly and half-aerial flight, the train glides across the tops of the houses. From his raised position the visitor gazes down upon the suburbs of London. The houses, in never-ending parade, like troops dressed by the right, line the eternal streets. He has left the soil behind; he has entered a country of houses – perhaps a continent.

I do not know how far I speak for others when I confess that for years I used to get a sinking feeling inside as the Irish Mail made its way into London. A feeling of dread – and of unbounded hope for ever betrayed. With this went an intensity of reverie seldom so stimulated at any other time. What traveller can read a book as the express, seemingly at increasing speed, makes for the heart of the great city? Thoughts, tilted upward to the stars, pass before the mind as swiftly as the flying scenes outside; daydreams dressed in the splendour of impossible triumph claim their slave; and in the rattle of the wheels is heard the music of the spheres.

2

Surprise in statement is the essential element in writing which lasts. It is that which separates literature from ordinary writing. The reader of literature is continually surprised at the turn of thought or the turn of phrase. The book is finished and laid aside. It can be taken up again. And yet again. The element of the unexpected gives it this power of resurrection. It makes it live. The book with the clichéd thought and phrase may have a bright existence for a little time, but when it dies it cannot be reborn. Only he whose thoughts and words are informed with this quality of surprise, this element of the unexpected, is entitled to hope that his work, like democracy, shall not perish from the earth.

Impressions and Reflections in London

The new work may not be loved at first sight. You may have to wait for its music, to hunt for its beauty. But the time comes when that new music and that new beauty are revealed, and treasured thenceforth for ever.

It is the same with cities. I can never forget how my first sight of New York transported me. Those illuminated cliffs sitting in the sea, shaped by the hand and shaped by the spirit. Those rooms that touched the clouds by day and were mixed with the stars by night. That Times Building in Broadway like a super-liner for ever cutting through the waves of traffic. My heart was raised. When I visit New York again perhaps I shall again be lifted up. It is also possible that I shall be let down. I shall know what to expect. I shall expect too much. The drastic picture in my mind may have assumed too great proportions. My second visit may be similar in experience to the re-reading of a thrilling book, the plot of which is known and the mystery revealed.

I do not say that a single visit to Paris, Rome, Stockholm, Budapest is enough to penetrate to their secret. But their beauties are so carefully emphasized that a minimum of surprise is felt by the spectator. With London it is different. The beauty of London, like the beauty of the English character itself, is not openly displayed. We continually come upon it unexpectedly. We stumble into it. We trip over it. We turn a corner down a narrow street, looking for a shop, and come upon a cathedral instead. Often we stop and almost gasp at the loveliness of a tree or a square surprisingly in our path. And when the gauzy blue veil is let down over London in the winter dusk we see beauty flowing and penetrating like water into ugly alleys, lanes, gullies, corners, dark recesses and labyrinthine agonies that spread before us. Then we grasp the secret of London: here we are brought close to the mystery of beauty itself, we see that it is not something that can be extraneously exhibited, but that like Love and Truth, it rises up inexhaustibly out of the agony of the world.

3

How then do homage to London? How call upon the Muse to guide me? For the mood cannot always be so affirmative. Often one is given over to less elevated feelings. To travel in the Tube, for instance, after breakfast, is to see London from a different perspective. It is truly to descend below in the scale of existence and to feel that such super-engineering is for submerged men. Perhaps it is the crowding that lowers the spirit. Or the silence of this sandwiched crowd of clean-handed sons of toil. They endure too much. No moan is heard even when they are crushed together so that no limb can move. I do not exaggerate that crush. One evening at the rush-hour, on getting in at Tottenham Court Road, I tripped and fell forward. Owing to the crowd I did not fall to the ground but remained stuck at an angle of forty-five degrees, and not until I had passed several stations was I able to regain my perpendicular. I have often wondered at the endurance of the people hanging up there on the straps like dead animals. Possibly they really like it, or cannot bear to be absent a moment longer than is absolutely necessary from their families. For they all insist upon coming home at the same moment, and hundreds who could go back by boat along the Thames in summer refuse to do so.

There is too little despair in this city. How seldom does anyone stop in his progress through the Walworth Road from the Elephant and Castle to Camberwell Green and give up – knowing that he has come to The End at last. How few bus-drivers suddenly go sane and mow down the multitude in the name of Life. How scarce are the eyes that even behold the uprooting or the tongues that contemn the spoliation. There is not enough despair. Therefore not enough hope. Only endurance.

But how magnificent it is! I once had occasion to go to a certain shop in Rotherhithe in the East End to buy a chair for someone who lived in the neighbourhood. The woman who owned the place said that she hadn't got the thing we wanted in stock, but suggested that we go with her to the wholesale dealer who lived not far away, she said, somewhere in Stepney.

We agreed to go, and after a great deal of waiting to start, at length started. Then a journey began. We arrived at Stepney – but not at our destination. We got into a bus: we got out of it. We got into a tram and out of it. We crossed streets and changed into more trams. We stood in the wind and waited for a tram, the right tram, to come. It was a cold and bloodless day, and at that hour in the afternoon when all meaning is withdrawn from the universe. And in the midst, our guide! – robust, heavily laden with body, absolutely calm, a timeless expression on her face. She was coming out to help us buy this chair, possibly going to make about sixpence profit, possibly not: but there she stood in the tram, waited by the kerb, walked through alleys – wholly indifferent to the world, to the awful waste of time, to the hopeless, scornful meanness of the streets!

As I stood about, empty and fallen, I began to see this woman in her true proportion. She was so perfectly subconscious that she might have been super-conscious. Without any mental strife she had reached that Indifference belonging to the highest philosophy: she had attained Nirvana without following the tenets of Buddhism. Her figure assumed gigantic shape before my eyes: in stone, ensculptured, I saw her stand by the kerb, example and prototype of the whole Cockney woman world whose unfailing and unfeeling shoulders support the atlas of injustice.

Our Odyssey continued. We arrived at our destination. The wholesale dealer didn't seem to want to sell his chairs: "not for sale" he kept repeating, "not for sale." But at length we ordered something and went out of the warehouse and parted from our guide upon whose countenance there had been laid no trace of the ruin and the ennui that had fallen upon us. Like a fish suspended in an element unknown to another species, she took her way, unheeding and unshaken.

In recalling that incident and reviving my memory of that woman, it seems to me that perhaps my remarks above concerning despair should be reserved for myself. It is all right for me to despair, but not for the inhabitants. Every environment produces its own particular form of life. These people grow out of these streets. It is their environment, their home, their needful atmosphere. Transport them elsewhere and they pine away. Take a London charwoman into the country and she will complain of the noise at night. "Them there birds," said one to me once, "was that noisy I couldn't sleep." In the daytime the lack of noise got her down, it "fair gave her the creeps." The disqualifications of the countryside being lack of pavements, shop-windows, cinemas, traffic and neighbours "'aving a good set-to." Nothing in England strikes me more than the existence of a new kind of person created by the towns. It is an interesting piece of progress. It makes those who insist that a "change of heart" is essential before people are changed, seem superficial. The moment a few people alter a large area of conditions, then the inhabitants of that area (who possess exactly the same slow evolutionary adaptability as animals) will begin to change accordingly. Probably this is pure Marxism – though it does *not* support the materialistic conception of history – which is a theory leaving out half the truth just as certainly as the unmaterialistic conception of history leaves out half the truth.

It is therefore not surprising to find that the people who live in slums do not regard them as such. They hate to hear the word used. This calls for a tactfulness amongst social reformers which is not always displayed. "A slum! What do you mean? Why, that's where I live!" was the indignant exclamation I once heard a workman give a well-meaning socialist who had been talking to him about "bringing down" the slums in a certain district. The average comfortable subscriber to The Times Book Club visualizes a slum as "a mass of congestion and confusion, hideous squalor and misery." Such places still exist; but the average "slum-dweller" in England would be really angry with such a description of his home.

An Irishman's England

What strikes me most about the East End is its *dinginess*. I have not found that the distinction holds good which claims wealth for the West End and poverty for the East End. The West End has area after area in which the inhabitants are quite as poor as in the East. But the whole of the Eastern part is poor, that is true. And its mark is this dirty dinginess which stretches on oceanically. The word End is wrong. There is no end that one can see – the Mile Un-ending Road is joined by a thousand tributaries which branch out in each direction through whole continents of dreariness. Yet here too we often stumble into Paradise. We continually come upon some graceful park or green nook around a church, really smiling shades in summer, filled with emerald and golden thoughts. And nowhere in London do the crocuses spring up with more promise in their lyric colours than in Southwark Park near Rotherhithe; and the same park contained the usual kind of island in its lake, reminding the onlooker of that far off Imaginary Place he yet may reach and of the peace he yet may find.

The East-ender himself is extremely respectable, the inside of his shop or house being similar in every way to the interiors of other houses all over London. His goal – a still greater respectability... As for Chinatown, the lack of villainy there now, the intense unromanticism of its streets, seem to point to the fact that respectable dinginess is to be the norm over vast areas of this extraordinary city.

One thing, however, marks off these areas from others – the gaiety of the children. Theirs is the freedom of the streets. They are exceptionally good-looking. Lack of money – save when it means really bad food – has no power over the happiness of childhood. I have seen plenty of unhappy children thrown upon the cushions of society; but unless my data is too meagre to generalize from, this eastern part of London is the place where I look for the most care-free children. But the difference between what they are and what they become, strikes one very hard, strikes one in the face. Never have I felt the tragedy of life's downward growth so strongly as during my many wanderings here. It is here that I have most sharply seen the brilliant, sun-like beams of youth going out. And when many a time I have seen a mother carrying an infant into a public-house in the evening, I have thought of a picture drawn by one of England's almighty bards. When recalling those ingenuous moments of our youth before we have learnt by use to slight the crimes and sorrows of the world, Wordsworth remembers a "lovely Boy" six months old whom he saw in London in a similar scene. "Upon a board," he says:

> Decked with refreshments had this child been placed
> *His* little stage the vast theatre,
> And there he sate surrounded with a throng
> Of chance spectators, chiefly dissolute men
> And shameless women, treated and caressed;
> Ate, drank, and with the fruit and glasses played,
> While oaths and laughter and indecent speech
> Were rife about him as the song of birds
> Contending after showers. The mother now
> Is fading out of memory, but I see
> The lovely Boy as I beheld him then
> Among the wretched and the falsely gay,
> Like one of those who walked with hair unsinged
> Amid the fiery furnace.
>
>   *   *   *   *   *   *   *
>
> But with its universal freight the tide
> Hath rolled along, and this bright innocent
> Mary! may now have lived till he could look
> With envy on thy nameless babe that sleeps
> Beside the mountain-chapel, undisturbed.

Though dinginess is the chief mark of the East End, nevertheless it is also here that we come upon the loftiest spectacle of the city. Few Londoners seem properly aware of the river below London Bridge. Yet the Docks make all other city gates appear hardly worth a visit. When I go and look at the Thames flowing between Tower Bridge and the West India Docks I am reminded of how Turner challenged his rival Claude from the grave. He left two of his own pictures to the nation on the express condition that they should always hang – as they are hanging today – beside two of Claude's in the National Gallery. His *Dido Building Carthage* and his *Sun Rising in Mist* stand over against Claude's *Isaac and Rebecca,* or *The Mill* and *Seaport: Queen of Sheba.* In Claude's pictures beauty is laid on with a trowel. Everything is ideal. The peaceful waves answer the smiling sky. The pastures are pastoral, the men are swains, the women are nymphs. The groups, in classic pose, are suspended in perpetual holiday. It is an idyll in Utopia, a state without the element of work or the conflict of life. Turner felt confident that if he gave an impression of reality, of fishermen at their daily work, posterity would recognize that he had not only painted something with meaning in it, but something with far more beauty than the pictures by Claude.

I think of this when I look at the Thames flowing through the Docks at full tide. There nothing has been built for the sake of beauty – neither the warehouses nor the steps nor the piers nor the cranes nor the barges and tugs and ships. Nothing is ideal. Romanticism does not come into it. Holidays, happiness, pleasures, peace are not in question. No conscious aesthetic effect has been aimed at. And yet…this is where we must go if we wish to attend at the mystery of beauty.[1]

4

I wonder whether any Englishman has ever understood the Chinese. The Chinese civilization was built up, and for centuries sustained, on the basis of *manners*. Courtesy counted more before God than good or evil (I like the story of the Chinaman who killed his son in the back-garden, and then apologized at great length for doing so, because the noise had disturbed his neighbour: he agreed that he should have done it elsewhere). English civilization is sustained on the basis of *ethics*. If the Church were removed from Ireland there might be a considerable increase in crime. Sweep every church out of England and there would not be the slightest difference in conduct. The ethical, moral, ideal soul of each man would guide him along the same as ever.

This makes for greatness. The English are a great people. It also makes for sadness. The English have an infinite capacity for not enjoying themselves. Their lack of vitality and exuberance are remarkable.

It has often been noticed how marvellous Londoners are at living in such a difficult crush – the way they oil the wheels of traffic, their habit of queueing up to take their turn for a bus or anything else, is justly famous. By never losing their tempers nor raising their voices nor loading their persons with unnecessary gestures, they set a fine example in civilized living. It is wonderful. But it makes them sad. They are sad in the bus, they are sad in the street, they are sad in the park. It is distressing to see them sitting or walking in Hyde Park so listless, so bowed down with care, so full of death. I have often thought how strange it is that sometimes the Authorities have thought it necessary to make special drives towards Greater Morality in the park. Little do they realize how small is the need for censorship of any kind in England – least of all for the attentions of Mr and Mrs Grundy!

To grasp the weakness of this people's vitality one must see them at their pleasures, their seaside resorts, their race-meetings, their fairs.

Every year at Easter an elaborate fair is held on Hampstead Heath. The latter is one of the most beautiful places in the world – and a typically

English gesture. It is not a heath. It is a big stretch of wood and meadow land, a piece of the ancient countryside with hills and vales. London beats upon it from all sides. This island is preserved with care. It is an intensely English utterance of ultimate sanity and fore-knowledge – as are also the other London isles like St James's Park, in itself a perpetual poem of beauty and peace. The overwhelming appeal of Nature at Hampstead Heath would be impossible without the existence of London beating upon it. The overwhelming appeal of London at Hampstead Heath would not be felt without the call of this Nature. From this green hill of hope we get a view of ultimate harmonies on a scale impossible to conceive elsewhere.

One Easter I stood on a slope in the blue of the evening haze. As I did so there reached me, not from above but from below, from beneath the soil, a strong, cold whiff of Spring, the *odour* of resurrection.

Passing on I rounded a corner and came upon a remarkable sight. In a small valley below dwelt a miniature city. It was glowing with stationary and moving lights, and sending up peals of gaiety and music. All was gladness down there, it seemed, a whoop of praise reaching to the sky. A thick mist existing nowhere else on the Heath had filled the valley and wrapped the town as in a shawl. The lights and movements in that mist belonged to fairyland and bore no relation to the life outside. The little city had evidently been let down from heaven in that shawl, and soon would be drawn up again.

Then I realized that it was connected with us. It was a fair, an Easter festival. It was a gathering of men, now again as in ancient times, to celebrate the pleasures of revival, the joy in our annual resurrection from the dead. It was a ceremony of value, a primal, pristine rite!

I went down from my Hill. I also went down from the high mood which that whiff of Spring had given me. Here was no festival – nor harmony, nor any joy. Though incongruity is the special mark of our era, entangling all our ways, I was surprised to see how *everything* here was pseudo, false with a fierce cynicism, flagrantly a lie, working for one object only – pennies. The music was mechanical, the boosting of each booth mechanical – the incongruity between what each booth-keeper promised and what he performed, an amazing farce.

What matter so long as the packed throng treats the business as a farce, an amusing game of make-belief? But how sadly the people took the joke! The miserable white faces of the London mob wore the hopeless expression of those who do not know what they are doing.

What was the meaning of this? I wondered. It must have some meaning or it could not go on. I looked closer. There was a "Wall of Death" – an item of terrifying danger. There were boats on wheels in which the occupants were bobbed up and down and knocked against each other enough to shake the life out of them. There were swings in which always one of the swingers was going higher than he or she could bear. There was a booth of whelks spread with vinegar and steeped in gall. Looking round, I perceived that the whole thing was designed to give the greatest unhappiness to the greatest number.

The meaning of the terrible scene dawned upon me. The nethermost desire here was *punishment*. These fairs unconsciously exist to inflict self-torture. It is the people's penance. It is the ancient spirit of flagellation that must needs find an outlet. It is the unconscious scourge and rod. It is asceticism in the raw. It is the monk-like hunger of men to turn away from their vileness and be redeemed from their sins!

I used to think that the dispirited look of the people might be due to the modern economic situation, the feeling of insecurity, and to the general lack of direction in the national life. It lies deeper. I find the same observation made by an Englishman for whom I have a particular partiality, Havelock Ellis, witness to the depth, the breadth and the clarity of the English mind at its best. Over sixty years ago he was at school on the high road from London to Epsom. On Derby Day the boys were permitted to watch the crowds driving to and from the meeting. "As long as I live," he writes, "I can never forget the people in that long melancholy procession of varied vehicles. Those pale, weary, draggled figures, their pathetically vulgar jokes, their hollow spasmodic gaiety, sadder than sorrow." And he goes on to speak of "how significant they are of our national temperament. For all our boasted practicality we are idealists always, and indeed that practicality is an outcome of our idealism, always pitched too high for any satisfaction that the world can yield, yet always compelled to seek it with ever more feverish energy. We have not the aptitude of the French to become artists in life and accept all its eventualities with good humour. We have not the aptitude of the Spanish to be children in life and to appreciate simply all its little things. We are so high-strung that there is nothing left for us but religion and the variegated preachers who form the spectacle, unique in the world, we see at the Marble Arch."

Those Hyde Park orators at the Marble Arch are already so world-famous that I need not call attention to them again. But I must not omit to emphasize that if one does not take their existence for granted, and if one comes upon the spectacle suddenly, it is felt as sufficiently remarkable. Nearly all the speakers are talking about religion – and the matter of their discourse is often incredibly puerile. There they stand, a long row of them, every day of every week, month after month and year after year, lifting up their voices. It is the voice of England that is being lifted up. Here, in the centre of their capital, the inarticulate craving at last finds a free outlet to arraign and to preach and to plead.

Lest anyone should think that the uplift element is oppressive I hasten to add that nothing can beat this oratory at entertainment value. Occasionally on my way to the Regal Cinema I have mingled with the crowd there, and finding this free show so entertaining I have not gone on to the cinema… And before leaving this subject, there is one man I would like to sketch in, for he very much held my attention and remains in my memory as symbolic of the whole show.

I had often wondered how a speaker had the courage to get started, beginning as he must, with an empty "house." I turned up one evening to find a beginner standing on his little ladder facing an audience composed of one. On each side of him a large crowd had gathered to hear another speaker. How then would he succeed in getting his audience? I wondered. He was a young man of about twenty-five, healthy-looking, and wearing open collar and shorts. "The test of any man's religion," he was shouting, "is in the personal life. But we cannot succeed in the personal life without Jesus Christ." At this point his audience of one, an elderly man, asked him a question: "What is your own job in life?" "I'm asked what my job in life is," shouted the speaker loudly, not looking at his questioner but addressing the large audience that had not yet gathered to hear him. "It is not a strictly relevant question. But I am what you see I am – a preacher. And I hold that if a man believes in his religion, well then it is up to him to pass it on to others. My first article of faith is…" and he launched on out of the question into an eloquent passage. I moved off to listen to other speakers, but always I found myself fascinatedly drawn back to watch this young man. He was not doing well. At one time his audience increased to three, but when I returned for the last time it had decreased again to one. He did not give up. Though very red and hot, he still preached on; and as I finally turned out of the Park away from the whole strange scene, I could still hear him answering his one heckler in clear loud tones to convince the great audience which was not there.

If the English do not show themselves to full advantage on occasions such as these, there are times when, en masse, they rise like no other people, to life's dramatic moments. They know how to bestow significance upon events which are everything or nothing precisely according to the spirit that goes out to meet them. The best example of this is the Two Minutes' Silence on

Armistice Day. You could never see a more truly English spectacle. The four ingredients so dear to this people's soul – Drama, Uplift, Idealism and a Great Sorrow – are here bountifully provided.

Perhaps to understand how real a thing it is to the English, one should have been in London on the first Armistice Day. On the afternoon of that day I happened to rise from underground at Trafalgar Square. I came into the centre of a London whose inhabitants probably never before have been in such a state of mind. Peace had not been signed, only an armistice; but everybody knew, without official confirmation, that the War was over. And instantly something broke in the people. In their millions they broke down. They made a scene.

I came up into the Square. The lions had practically disappeared – all except their heads had sunk beneath the crowd. Every single person was doing two things: shouting and waving at least one arm. A thin lane left room for traffic which slowly moved forward. The people were not in any of the vehicles, they were *on* them. Taxis and private cars had no one inside them, but four or five men and girls stood on the roofs shouting and waving – and everyone seemed to have got hold of a flag to wave. Those who saw this scene can scarcely recall it even now without a moistening of the eyes and a raising up of the hair.

I walked down Whitehall. A man took his bowler hat and executed a neat drop-kick with it towards Downing Street. A suburban young lady kissed a stranger. In a restaurant I saw an elderly gentleman, slightly the better for drink, going round from table to table and gently laying his lips upon the crown of all bare heads – an office which was nowhere ill-received. Hour after hour and day after day passed and yet there was no abatement of this frenzied and unfenced emotion.

Since then I have witnessed many Armistice Days. Standing again at Trafalgar Square I have seen the multitude – this time silent, this time still. Big Ben strikes eleven o'clock: every vehicle stops, every noise ceases. Silence moves across like a wave of peace. In the extraordinary suspension, a thousand pigeons who have been perching in wreaths round the Pillar, fearing some superlative catastrophe, fly outwards wheeling round and round in panic, theirs the only movement and the flapping of their wings the only noise over the great jungle of rooted men. I have seen the busiest streets in London turned into cathedral aisles of prayer. I have seen, most impressive of all, the side street in which the single workman bares his head and halts his spade – with no crowd to prompt him. The scene is always too big to grasp; but I know that in this country those two minutes are made more lofty in their abasement than any hour of joy and pride.

To fail to see this greatness is to fail in understanding; to have the heart of lead and the eye of stone. The heroism of the men who fought and of the men who fell, may be doubtful, even utterly fantastic when we consider what their work was (to whatever nation belonging). The world may have betrayed and wasted them, but they themselves betrayed and laid waste the world. They may have been victims of folly and sin, but their obedience meant the increase of sin and folly. Those women who on Armistice Day are seen selling poppies are often the same women who gave white feathers to the men who delayed at first to rush to the slaughtering – women who doubtless would exchange the poppies for feathers again tomorrow if the occasion arose. We may grant all this. But Armistice Day is great precisely because these facts are transcended for two minutes. That is a long time for the achievement of a concentrated and continuous religious moment. This is religion: this is art in action – if either in their purity have ever been shared and created by a multitude. For two minutes all men are brothers thinking a single thought and joined together with one hope. For two minutes they commit no evil. For two minutes every gracious desire and every adorable ideal uppermost in the hearts of the English people receive the sure and certain promise of fulfilment. For two minutes there is perfect peace.

No nation can achieve this kind of art without fumbling or staining it, save the English. Here they are masters. In this way they alone are capable of giving expression, en masse, to that element of goodness in human nature which we are still afraid to trust.

They very much enjoy the creation of such an atmosphere. I have suggested above that they are not good at being happy. But one must make the reservation that they love nothing better than a living drama if it moves in a homely, moral field, and if they have created it themselves on a great national scale; and they do really enjoy and let go of themselves when the activities of Royalty provide the material for that drama. It is necessary to make more than a mere reservation, and to affirm that in the building up of these national dramas and morality plays they are not only unsurpassed but they stand alone in their supremacy. Further, in the technical execution of the work they set a standard which it would be impossible to find excelled elsewhere.

The passing of George V appeared to me at the time, and appears to me still, as the most artistic performance in the history of all monarchies. Nor is it possible to conceive of any Broadcasting Corporation that could have met the situation with an equal dignity or a more finished art than that displayed by the BBC. For those who were listening-in from the country it could not fail to be as moving as a great play, as indeed it was, a magnificent Last Act, staged from Heaven and produced by the Announcer on earth.

However much the BBC may have gone to extremes, in a thoroughly English way, after the death, the announcement of the dying was masterly work. The long silence when the News was due, and then at last the Voice – "This is London. The following bulletin has been received from Sandringham – *The King's life is moving peacefully towards its close*. Another announcement will be made at 10 p.m." Then precisely the same words at 10 p.m., and again at 10.15, at 10.30, at 10.45, at 11p.m., at 11.15, at 11.30, at 11.45, till, as Big Ben strikes midnight, the King expires.

It was tremendous. In company with a multitude of others drawn together by means of the wireless, I bent my thoughts upon this single mystery, and sat in silence waiting for the end. One could feel the nation focusing upon this thing. Here was an unexampled concentration upon one event. The concert, the talk, the play, the dance tune, the news of the world's – all silenced for the one Announcement: "This is London" (the world's centre). "The following bulletin has been received from Sandringham: *The King's life is moving peacefully towards its close*." And thus, the nation, in public places, in family groups, in lonely rooms, unified with that single thought stood waiting for the end.

It was moving, as perhaps only the unragged purity of great art can move us. Nor could I fail to be touched subsequently when, walking in the public way, I beheld the people still living in the drama and clothed with the poetry of grief. "We Mourn Our Beloved King" I read over the portal of a tobacconist's shop. "We Grieve Not As They Who Mourn Without Hope" was chalked on the window of a shoemaker. "I feel as if I had lost a father," said a man to me selling socks. And the lying-in-state must have commanded the longest queue in the history of the world.

But it was not till I entered the suburban railway carriage that I really made contact with a member of the audience and was privileged to hold converse with one of His Majesty's real subjects. I was alone in the carriage when at Knockholt a little man got in – a grey, old-young, little clerky man with a washed-away pale face almost the colour of an old sheet. There are two occasions when an Englishman will speak to a stranger in the railway carriage: when the subject of cruelty to animals crops up, and on the Death of Kings. So he immediately addressed me, saying: "Sir, our Beloved King has taken his last journey today" (for it was the Thursday when he had been brought to Westminster Hall). "Not long ago," he continued, "I took a snapshot of His Majesty on the balcony of Buckingham Palace – I treasure that, I treasure that!" Instantly rising to the occasion, I replied: "Sir, in the past and up till modern times it has been possible for a king to be one of four things: he could be a Ruler or a Conqueror or an Emperor or a Tyrant, according to his taste or strength. None of these rôles is now possible. Unless a king has the genius to create a new rôle he is washed out or kicked out. Alone amongst all latter-day sovereigns George V had the genius to create a new rôle, he became – a Father. Not a false and insincere Father like the Tsars of Russia, but a real one who rejoiced in the joy and shared in the sorrows of his people. But, mark you," I continued with emphasis, "such a new rôle could not have been created by guile, it could not have been created by mere cleverness, nor even by the desire to be a Father. It was created almost unconsciously by a *good man*, and was accepted by the people because he was good." These words were received by my companion with ill-concealed emotion. He rose higher to the occasion: plucking at his collar a bit, nervously coughing off the audacity of his utterance, he jerked out: "I – er – think that he was the greatest man – since Jesus Christ."

At the next station he got out, warmly shaking me by the hand. I gazed after him, feeling that this had been more than a mere episode and incident – that it provided a symbol for all that strange week. I gaze after him still, that fantastic little citizen whom I shall never really comprehend, and into whose theatre I may not enter.

And if the drama of the death of George V was a magnificent performance all round, the drama of his son's abdication was stupendous. These works, both performed in the same year, are surely a vindication and a justification of English Monarchy that should hold good for all time.

Entering the theatre for a whole week to watch this play called "The Crisis" they escaped from the real world. What they saw had no meaning, no roots in the real issues of the day, it had nothing that could substantially touch their lives. It was a play. But it was absorbing. It held attention. The world outside did indeed cease to exist for one whole thrilled week, and it may well be doubted whether any other sovereign ever achieved so much for his people.

5

In London one continually comes upon a mews. A thin alley leads off the street to a court where horses used to be stabled. They are not stabled there now. To an Irishman brought up with horses, these places raise painfully romantic reflections.

One day I was passing a mews. At the far end of the alley I saw a man with a duster in his hand wiping down the bonnet of a motor car which was protruding from the one-time stable. Then, exactly as if I were in a cinema witnessing a splendidly imaginative fade-out, I saw in my mind's eye this man fade out and in his place stand a groom, also with a cloth in his hand – wiping down a horse.

I stuck there in the opening as if I had seen a vision – so clear was the picture before my eyes.

I passed on – back again into the London to which I belong, the London of the Chauffeur Age. The worst of it is there is something a bit depressing about chauffeurs. Something almost sub about them. Not that there was anything super about grooms. But one feels drawn to a groom and not to a chauffeur. It is the vital question of the human touch, I suppose – or, rather, the horse-touch humanized the groom, brought him into contact with a living thing.

There were no machines at all in the place in Ireland where I was brought up. And when I came to England for the first time I was old enough to be able to note the way in which too much dealing with machines has an unbalancing effect upon human beings. If you tread on a man's toe in the street or run into him by mistake, he will take it with good humour and good manners. Meet the same man later in a car and do something – anything – which annoys him, and he will immediately howl abuse at you like an animal. This is a phenomenon which I have never been able to get accustomed to – the sub-human, high-pitched offensiveness of the complete stranger who shares some motor mishap with you. In smaller ways also, people go slightly mad when they come near a car. A man leaves his room closing the door behind him quietly like a sane person. But he *slams* the door of his car. He doesn't ask himself whether it is any more necessary for him to do this than for a porter to bang the carriage doors of a train (actually it isn't necessary in either case), he just does so because he has suddenly become slightly unbalanced by proximity to the machine. Even telephones have a strange effect. If someone knocks at a door the owner of the room or house goes to it in a leisurely fashion and opens it. But people *run* to a telephone, at the risk of breaking one or more of their limbs going down the stairs, while it is an unheard of thing for anyone to finish what he is saying to you if the telephone rings.

However, I must not digress or pretend that these things are peculiar to England alone. For even when so ancient an instrument as a whistle comes into relation with a machine, madness amongst the people around follows in any country. I hear a whistle in the garden. Right – I have simply heard a whistle, and I go on with my tea. I enter a station refreshment room. My train goes at 7.30. It is now 7.10. At 7.15 I hear a whistle outside. I instantly put down my cup of tea, leave my bun unfinished and rush to the door – having temporarily lost my reason.

The thing that strikes me most about the London traffic is its silence. One day I was sitting in a car in a hold-up at the gates which lead out of Hyde Park to the main road in front and to the right to the Albert Memorial (all memorial and no Albert). A very long line of cars passed in front. They made scarcely any noise – and the cars waiting in the block made as little. I closed my eyes. I might have been in the middle of the countryside. Hearing nothing louder than the murmur of innumerable bees.

Every year there are more and more cars, but owing to their modern workmanship they make less and less noise. The Underground also is becoming silent. In some places the traffic is still very loud, and in an island park you can still hear a rolling rumbling roar around; but peace is undoubtedly descending, for we must also remember that the more traffic there is the more it gets jammed, until in many places cars assume the nature of rooms in the street on unmoving wheels – residences which are necessarily silent. (Hence many rich London people are forced to live a large part of their lives five in one room.)

In view of this the fate of the bicycle in London is most surprising. It was and remains indisputably the greatest invention of man. Yet no gentleman will be seen using one in London now. It is amazing. I may thank God that in this I am not as other men, and for some years in London I made the bicycle my chief means of transport. I was able to go everywhere with ease, speed and comfort. A bicycle will take one anywhere. I once rode over the frozen Serpentine when it wouldn't hold skaters.

6

Outside the Shaftesbury Theatre a street-entertainer was attempting to hold the attention of a queue. He was an elderly man. I had seen him several times before at various places, but had never been able to wait long enough to follow out the dénouement of his trick – something to do with a bottle, and pathetically hopeless.

Here he was doing it again at this turning leading down to Leicester Square. Apparently he was infringing the law in some way – traffic-obstruction no doubt – for a policeman slowly approached the scene.

The man saw him coming and went on with his entertainment, but with the air of one who might at any moment be stopped.

The policeman approached, in no hurry. On arriving he said nothing; he did not even look at anything particular. Unferociously, and with tremendous lack of haste, he took up a position directly behind the man. He was very tall, a cliff. He made no gesture, uttered no word: he stood looking down at the man below, not in any anger, nor the slightest sorrow, and yet with sympathy – a Force, impregnable, beyond entreaty or reproach.

The entertainer gradually became paralysed. He stopped building up his trick, and looking round over his shoulder seemed about to make some protest or appeal to this Presence behind who still stood absolutely motionless, silent, his head high up there looking straight ahead, thinking what thoughts?

At last the man turned away his cringing, miserably afraid face, picked up his bottle, and moved off.

Thus I hasten to preserve the convention and make my bow to the London policeman before proceeding further. I am happy to do so. He is not quite so pleasant as the Irish policeman – except when he happens to be an Irishman – but he certainly is "wonderful." He is truly a Force. He is the most English thing on earth. If anyone does anything unEnglish in this country, the injured party simply calls in a policeman. Elsewhere he would make matters worse. Here he bestows peace.

He never needs to raise his voice, far less an explosive weapon. It is only necessary for him to appear – and order is restored. Many a London policeman has reminded me of the Chinese Emperor, Shun, who only had to sit on his throne, with his face turned towards the South, and there was perfect harmony on earth.

For he gives personal expression to the English profound respect for law. He bathes in the support of a whole nation. He is legality. He is the guardian of morality. He is respectability walking in their midst. He is the image of their desire.

If we want an example of the English policeman at his best and most English, we know where and when to look. We watch a communist demonstration or the like. I will always remember the first time I witnessed this. A long Red procession was making its way from London Bridge to Hyde Park. It had to pass across the Exchange, all the way up Holborn and Oxford Street, in fact along the most crowded parts of London. But a large number of policemen *escorted them thither*. The traffic was held up for them as if Royalty were passing.

I could believe my eyes – for this was England. Here were the guardians of society protecting and assisting and holding up the traffic so that the would-be destroyers of society could march into Hyde Park to make a revolutionary demonstration.

Since then I have watched many similar scenes of police assistance given to facilitate the activities of those who are against the present social order. Often Hunger Marchers are joined by hundreds of policemen who march with them through the streets.

This is not cunning: it is *english* – a special thing not capable of being handed from one nation having it to another nation not having it. It belongs only here – and its symbol is the unarmed policeman.

7

I once met a man walking up Charing Cross Road accompanied by a small elephant. There was a certain element of incongruity in this spectacle, one might even call it surprising. But what surprised me more than the elephant and its companion was the minimum of attention which they attracted. To say that no one took any notice of them would be an understatement. A good many passers-by turned round and stared, while some stopped and gazed after the pair. But they created little comment and no stir.

The most delightful thing about London is that nobody minds what anyone does or says – within the bounds of morality. There is an individual freedom about the place which fittingly symbolizes the English spirit. Barrie is held to have said that the chief thing about London is that you can eat a bun in the street without drawing attention to yourself. You need not wear a hat. No garb is laughed at: a man clothed in the flowing robes of a Franciscan Friar with long hair down his neck will occasion as little surprise as a parrot perched on someone's shoulder – while during a heatwave there is such an extremity of unconventionality as to scandalize many foreigners who do not understand the effect which a few days' continuous sunshine has upon English people. Anyone may talk to himself aloud without notice: indeed, the number of persons who smile and chat to themselves alone as they walk through the streets makes up for their reserve when they get together.

On the other hand, a welcome is given to anyone who wishes to draw a crowd. Street-entertainers, some of whom perform nothing more elaborate than the tearing across of a telephone directory, can gather the most patient and good-natured audiences. Prophets who wish to give their message in the street easily find a following. The pavement artist has his best chance here. And at the same time the incongruous and crushing comment in the spectacle of able-bodied men selling fluffy, jumping toys on the kerbs of the rich pavements, makes no one pause.

When the image of London rises before me all these things form part of it. But one thing more than these – the street singers. In many districts I have seen and heard musicians and singers banding together with so much dignity and power of expression that their very act has been a triumph and has raised up my heart even at the moment when it was most cast down. I call to mind especially one band of Welsh miners who had taken up their position in the full and noisy Holborn quarter. As I passed one day I saw them marching slowly onwards singing. At first their voices were drowned by the traffic. Then they rose above the roar. Their song conquered the clamour. They climbed above it in a swelling chorus. I could not see them now, for they got mixed up with the crowd at the other side of the street, but I still heard their voices. With triumphant irony, these men who had been thrown aside by society, neglected and betrayed, were singing with a power and beauty that raised them high above the corruption and the wrong!

However, neither this nor anything else disturbs or surprises the Londoner. Even when Nature refuses an elementary office and the next day does not dawn and night follows the night, he still goes about his business as if all were in order. The mere fact that there is darkness when there should be light does not derange his equanimity. Indeed, he enjoys it. I enjoy it myself, I confess. This happens when the famous London fog forms above the city instead of in it. It is a rather rare occurrence, but it holds the attention. A lid of fog too thick to be penetrated by the light of the sun is laid over the town about the height of a church spire from the streets. Thus at ten o'clock in the morning it is as dark as at ten o'clock in the evening. The lights are lit and everyone carries on in a city of continuous night.

But when this lid descends to the streets, then even the Londoner finds life difficult. I have never seen one of those fogs when it is said that "you cannot see your hand in front of you." It is sufficiently intriguing when you cannot see across the road. Strange things happen. You alight from a car to look for the kerb – the car disappears and you cannot find it again. A lamp, far away like a light-house in the sky, next second strikes against you. A moving cliff hung with lights, suddenly shaped from the insubstantial mist like an act of creation on the First Day, collides against your own trembling barque. You have re-entered, it seems, an earlier period in the earth's history, and may even have become a wanderer in the Immense Inane.

The reader must consult heavier volumes than this to find out the scientific cause of these fogs – whether due entirely to the smoke or to changes of temperature in the moist atmosphere. As I feel pretty sure that smoke has less to do with it than natural causes, I dare say it will remain one of the characteristics of London. I hope so. For the same cause is probably responsible for the hazy blue light, the gauzy veil of blue through which one walks in the dusk. I would call that the most movingly lovely thing in the world. It melts the mind. I always miss it when I go away from London. I do not forget the innumerable blues of the Celtic scene, I know what it is to be cut off from those visionary roads and high paradises that are lost in that light. But this blue is not inferior. It joins God and Man, refusing the immeasurable melancholy of manless beauty. When, in the Bloomsbury Squares, I see hanging in that blue, interwoven with that gauze, light as air, substantial as rock, the little balls on the plane-tree's tracery – when I see them scriptured in the dusk of the cold winter sky – then I know that London has claimed me for her own.

8

When revolutions occur without there being a Revolution, or when a piece of pure communism is established without any battle for it, then no one realizes that the thing has happened. In an eccentric and revolutionary country like England we see many examples of this. The best illustration which the world can show of pure communism within the limited sphere of receiving intellectual food is provided by the British Museum Reading Room.

Admission is free into this remarkable library in the centre of London. It is open to every race and to all sexes. No distinction is made between the rich and the poor, the clever and the stupid, the real and the fake, the industrious and the lazy, the believer and the atheist, the conservative and the rebel – all alike receive the same goods for *nothing*, and the same consideration if they seek assistance from the officials who seem to take a special pleasure in courteous attention. It is, in my experience, the most perfect example of that English tolerance which delights to welcome "all shades of opinion" and to give "fair play" to the champions of all causes. Whatever a man's aim may be, this gate of truth is thrown open to him so generously and so genuinely that when, for instance, Lenin had finished studying the work of a former reader called Karl Marx, he was in a position to rise from Seat L.13, leave the library and stand a whole Empire on its head (from the English point of view) and to cut off the heads of those who did not like that position.

In this Reading Room it is officially claimed that you can get out any book written by any person in any country in any age. This cannot be true. But the fact remains that any book which you look up in the catalogue (W B Yeats said that he had to give up coming to the Museum because these catalogues were too heavy to lift) is nearly always there. The Room is circular. From the balcony it looks like a giant wheel with the readers at their desks for spokes, and the inner circle of catalogues for the hub. Radiating under and outwards from this Wheel That Turns Not Round stretch forty miles of book-shelves – a honeycomb of knowledge, a mine of books. "All shades of opinion are welcomed here": shades indeed, and ghosts, and apparitions of opinion wandering and reverberating through the everlasting corridors of prose!

It is typical of England that though she cares less for the things of the mind than any other civilized nation, she should have erected the best library in the world (this country is like that in everything). The English themselves do not think much of the place. To them appearance means everything. They cannot see that what goes on in the Reading Room may be more fundamentally *active* than the proceedings down the street in the House of Commons. They think that in the beginning is the Act. They will not acknowledge that in the beginning is the Word. The Word that sows the seed may not be seen. It works underneath the ground, and those who convey it may be clothed in shabbiness and penury. Our deepest desires are put into ideas, our ideas into theories and programmes – until at last the great movements advance and are executed well or badly by the MPs and the PMs who occupy the seats of power. But such transcendentalism is hateful to the English or to the Scottish mind. Even their own mystics gibe at the Museum Library. Edward Carpenter – one of those gracious flowers of English culture envied by all nations – could not avoid his joke at its expense. "What is it, such a library?" he exclaimed. "It is the homage of industrious dullness to the human soul." And again:

"How lovely!
All the myriad books – well-nigh two millions of volumes – the interminable iron galleries, the forty miles or so of closely-packed shelves;
The immense catalogue – itself a small library – of over a thousand volumes;

* * * * * * *

The mountain-peaks of literature, and the myriads of lesser hills and shoulders and points – the mole-hills and grass-blades even;

* * * * * * *

How lovely!
To think there are all these books – and one need not read them."

Hence most of the people who make profitable use of the Reading Room are foreigners – the stuffy atmosphere (as he calls it) is too much for the robust, open-the-window Englishman who is content to come and sip from the honeycomb now and then (every eminent man of letters seems to have done this one time or another), though occasionally a person like Samuel Butler, who routined every hour of his day, makes it into a permanent study. The distinguished habitués nearly all come from foreign countries – to which they seldom return. The English habitués are extinguished almost as human beings – which is partly due to the fact that with unsurpassed British thoughtlessness as to the aim of the Library the authorities close it at six p.m., just as the authorities of the Church of England, with unsurpassed British thoughtlessness as to the aim of a church, close St Paul's Cathedral at six p.m. lest anyone instead of rushing home should commit the indiscretion of going in to pray.

For some years my own work brought me into intimate touch with this Reading Room, and I confess that I grew very fond of it. I used to reach it in time to secure a seat on the edge of one of the spokes of the wheel so as to have no one on my right (you never see the man opposite, for a splendid English hedge of wood shields you off from him). There I would often sit all day, sometimes without going out for food. The lack of movement used to make me so chilly that at last, putting my overcoat over my shoulders and half-submerging my head, I probably almost disappeared as a person.

Thus I was able to understand the appeal which this place made to the poor English habitués. For them it is a workhouse – in the sense in which that word is used in England, an asylum, a retreat from the work of the outside world. One day, having gone through the swing-doors into the short corridor leading to the Reading Room, I paused, struck by a figure stooping over the hot-water pipes which at one time were in that passage. He was meagre of body, utterly slighted by Nature; his back almost a hump, his shoulders falling away at a hopeless angle, covered by a grey thin overcoat beyond death itself; trousers with beggary in every fold, as if upheld by no kind of braces, creased his legs; a long piece of string dangled from the lining of a pocket; his broken-down hat was well over the forehead and half over the face, while shivering grey hair miserably fell behind. He stood stooping over the pipes, neither moving nor turning his mouse-like face to left or right. I was glad to see him there instead of in a less dignified workhouse. He was not an exceptional figure. An even greater decay had settled upon another intellectual tramp who once, sitting beside me, rose, went to the shelves and raising his ragged arms addressed the books in half-silent exhortation. These derelict men are a special feature of the Library, though all are not quite so overthrown. I took the following note concerning one who had obviously found his home at last: "The Reading Room would be unthinkable without him. He is poor, he is faded, he is sadly happy. He comes early, he goes at the last minute. Often he sleeps. Often he stands outside on the steps of the Museum in vague gaze. He is in no haste. He is without purpose; it is impossible to believe that he is getting anywhere in his studies. Clearly he is lost. From what does he fly? And when the cruel door closes whither does he go? Here, at any rate, from nine to six, he is not lost. This is his home, his asylum, his earthly paradise; for him here there is sure and certain peace; in this place he will keep watch until he dies – nay, in this harbour he cannot die, for outside it he does not exist. He shall be found here from generation to generation and from age to age."

There are more impressive immortals also suspended in this Room. Men who must surely be getting somewhere. I have only known this Museum off and on for a trifling fourteen years, but enough perhaps to allow me to appreciate the labours of those permanent students who have been taking notes every day for some forty years. I have never not seen a certain tall, thin, serene dark man (a foreigner) walk in, turn to the right at the entrance and go to the same chair – he is obviously accomplishing something, his upright carriage and perpetual half-smile reflect his progress. The same is true of the man whom I would call the Colossal Priest. No one has ever not seen him there, summer, winter, autumn, spring. You leave this Museum for a long time, you travel into a far country. You return. And there, as if only an hour had passed, is the Great Priest walking in or out of the Room. His garments are those of some French ecclesiastical personage. His proportions are elephantine. His extremely large head, crowned with a little cap, looks extremely small on a body that can be second to none in weight. As the years pass he becomes ever more prodigious, his stomach advancing still further to the front. His body divides him from his books by an expanse that might make comfortable reading difficult, but his eyes are good and he sees across the distance. Though sometimes found asleep, his general operations are impressive, he knows what he is doing, and piles his desk high with tier after tier of books. Sooner or later he will complete a superlative scholastic work, and at last return to his own country with the mightiest tome the world has ever seen!

Around this drastic presence, this rock of ages, there cling and grow and wither the lesser perennials. In the outside world crisis follows crisis, while away from it all in the Reading Room a small thin man takes innumerable notes in microscopic note-books until at last he walks with his head bent forward at a shocking angle; while a strange frock-coated gentleman who is unable to work for more than a quarter of an hour at a stretch without getting up and talking to someone, carries out work on Chinese texts; while a negro studies Latin grammar; while a faded beauty writes a novel; while an old woman reads with her eyes so near the print that her forehead rests on the page.

The more eccentric readers are not so constant in attendance. One seldom sees the man who tried to come in clothed only in a loin-cloth; or the man who went out carrying one of the chairs on his back; or the reader wearing rubber gloves and with a perforated enamelled mug strapped over his mouth; or the heavily veiled lady who used to raise her veil at intervals to stick a piece of stamp-paper on the end of her nose. But they are not excluded. The British genius in tolerance which shines like the sun upon the good and the evil thing, not only recognizes that eccentricity is necessary to the ultimate harmony of the world, but realizes that if knowledge is only made accessible then those who know how to use it will use it. There are not a few such always in that Reading Room, though they may not be the most conspicuous. They possess the secret of how to turn knowledge into power – and if only one out of every ten of these young men succeeds in his blazing ambition, the result is justified. And occasionally in that room it is their privilege to look up and see the serene and noble countenance of a Havelock Ellis or a G K Chesterton, masters of learning who have so magnificently added to their country's House of Honour and Fame.

9

I stood near the Carreras Factory at Camden Town at six p.m. and watched the girls come out. It seemed that they would never cease to flow from that door. And as I gazed at the never-ending march of artificial silk stockings it appeared to me that the factory was turning out these girls rather than other goods.

In a sense I was right. The advent of the machines in the last century meant also the advent of thousands more children. Wherever a machine appeared babies were born.

This aspect of industrialism has always seemed to me the worst. I come from a country which was saved by England from over-industrialism. This great benefit which was conferred upon us is even more clear today when the whole population of Ireland is not more than that of London – where one so often feels utterly submerged in an ocean of struggling men and more women. To the outsider the population of England appears in the light of an obvious catastrophe and to herald the end of culture. The tiny island is asked to hold in comfort a population out of all proportion to its seating capacity.

The people are not evenly distributed over it: eighty per cent are said to live packed up in the towns which are as unpleasant as the country is lovely. The thing seems preposterous. Indeed it is so bad that when the population shows signs of decreasing, a wail goes up from the second-rate experts that the nation is in danger! And the non-experts actually repeat the cry. In the squash they have forgotten that the command, "Increase and multiply!" was given to a nation which at that time consisted of four people.

10

A last glimpse before we move outward from London. A scene not lacking in those elements which used to appeal to the adventurous, nature-conquering and nature-loving hearts of Englishmen. Piccadilly Circus – when it shrinks.

No one loves it more than I do when it shines and triumphs in its own right. I like to look up in the evening and see the advertisements, mighty in the service of Mammon, illuminating the empyrean; and to look down, if it is raining, at their reflection in the streets that seem as water. To the profound eye the spectacle is seen to be, in its ultimate reality, what the Indians call *Lila*, sport. It is a play, a game, a lyric. If we rest our minds one remove higher than intellectual knowledge and sophistication, we see that it is not for money's sake, not for Bovril's sake or Craven A's sake, that the lights revolve in ceaseless chase; but for the sake of fun – and if for the sake of money, then for the sake of that which in itself is fantastic in its fairy-power. ... And so there is no place where I am more content to stand than here, where those things which are superficial reflect those things which are deep, and where that which is temporal directs my gaze towards that which is eternal.

Occasionally Piccadilly presents another spectacle, inviting other trains of thought which bring us back to the elements. It sometimes happens that a violent hurricane accompanied by a cloud-burst sweeps down upon London. At such moments it is worth being at Piccadilly. I have seen the Circus swept clean of human beings, even of cars. Overcoats, hats, umbrellas proving a hopeless protection against the wind and the torrent, everyone dashes for cover – and the Circus is given back to Nature. I have seen the wind, in sudden Atlantic fury, blow a woman, in all the plumes of her sophistication, from Upper to Lower Regent Street. I have seen a taxi twiddled round like a toy. For a few brief moments, prophetic of an ultimate day, Nature has returned and Man has retired.

---

1 For detailed description of the Docks at Rotherhithe see *The Sounding Cataract* (Cassell).

2

IMPRESSIONS AND REFLECTIONS IN THE COUNTRY

We move outward from London. In doing so we need not dwell upon the existence of the suburbs. There are worse places. And there are worse people than the suburbanites. Before they marry, the majority are much the same as other people, aspiring and inspired. Before marriage, that is.

Beyond the suburbs there are the houses which have just been built and which will later achieve the status of suburb – new, bright, detached and half-detached houses working their way out into the fields and gradually creating streets and crescents. To the eye of the onlooker it would seem that no human being could conceivably take a house there; that he who lived in such a place must for ever be surrounded by a desert of barren thoughts.

So one would think. But people do take them. Not because they belong to a different species of humanity, but because they somehow feel that the houses they take are the last ones and that the field in front will remain a field. They are too weakly human! That field soon changes into a row of houses, and the brook into a petrol station. But they trustfully refuse to imagine it. I know people in Forest Hill, Clapham and Croydon who all thought that their lovely view and the old tree would remain. That is how the continent of London has spread – because people believed that it could not possibly spread any further.

However, I am really working my way towards a description of something else which calls for an historian. It would be a pity if no record were made of it. *Near* London the effect of the city can be something truly sordid.

Certain places in the country proper, but within easy reach of London, are blighted and stained so low as to amount to a betrayal of the human spirit.

I have had occasion to visit one such place many times, and I would call it "The Blighted Valley." It is twenty miles from London – a charming natural cleft in the hills with fields and woods and copses. Yet to go there is to walk through the valley of the shadow. Death is there. Not the Angel of Death in his triumphal car scattering the abominable Sentence and completing the last Act; but slow death while yet in life, a curse from above, a withering from below, a blight upon the ground.

Here is the first dwelling. It looks like, and probably is, a railway carriage come to its last station. An old man stands in the garden with a fork. Never have I beheld a more decayed being outside a hospital. His face is green, his body thin as a pencil, his clothes like damp mould upon a tree. He is past all doctoring, almost a ghost. He jabs his fork into the stony ground to no purpose. He will not survive ten minutes more.

I pass to the next house. Scattered round it in an area of about fifty square yards are numerous creosoted sheds. In between them are two or three carcases of motor cars slowly sinking into the earth. Piles of wire-entanglement and pieces of corrugated iron roofing lie on the ground. Two goats are endeavouring to derive sustenance from grass which is dirty with oil and thick with nuts and screws. One pig pokes about looking remarkably ill at ease. Of human beings there is neither sight nor sound.

Further on I come to another little garden gate. But what is this behind it? A dozen yellow asphalt pillars arranged by pairs in a row. Evidently it is the long-since-neglected foundation for an archway, an aesthetic effect. One rose-tree clings to one pillar. This attempted archway leads nowhere: it stops dead, and you must cross a waste field of slag-heaps before you come to a crouching bungalow. Standing there gauntly in the field, abandoned by man and flower, this archway is a more surprising phenomenon than the Marble Arch; and it is painful to think of the lack of pleasure it must have given to those who conceived it, to those who made it, and to those who look upon it.

I arrive at the next house, the next shack, the next cabin. It might be Australia. People pioneering out into the wild. But there everyone would be preparing to live: here they have come to die. The whole place seems to say – This is the end: life has come to this: it is finished: *finitum est.*

What is this place? Surely last time I passed, a bungalow was here. It has gone. The owners have taken it away with their other belongings. I remember them – two old actors who got parts in Christmas pantomimes, wrecked on this shore.

The next place is deserted, no movement of life ever seems to happen there – a plague-stricken house. The neighbouring ghostly dwelling is guarded by two yelping dogs. And further on I come across two people sitting by a fire in their garden. I look at them, they look at me – as if across the river of oblivion.

What next? A high and black-walled building, each window of which is broken and stuffed with sacking, and with yet another shed sheltering half a cart upon which hangs a dissolving coat – and neither man nor boy is seen. A step further and I am opposite another frightful and affrighting house, with a garden of bathing boxes. I turn my eyes away only to see on the other side of the hedge a still more shivering sight of sorrow and decadence with a space in front strewn with the wreckage of machinery like hopes betrayed.

Thus do we pass through a valley of the shadow of death without any hope that it may lead to a celestial city. There is no hope at all. It is beyond melancholy; it is far too deep a sadness for tears or mourning. The birds sing and nature shines here; but one longs for the town street with all the gadgets of modern civilization or for the desolations that are not desolating as on the Western bog with its melancholy in which there is a song however mournful. But here vitality, mentality, spirituality and sociality have been *sucked* away. Such things happen near London. It is one of the effects of the over-swollen metropolis. But let us forget it.

2

It is easy to forget it. It is even easy to forget London. That is a point Londoners might do well to remember.

Going in certain directions, there comes a point when the atmosphere of London is no longer felt, when the towns of England are not thought of as possible realities. At last we have reached the ancient soil.

Ireland has been called the Emerald Isle. It has never struck me as a good colour description of Ireland as a whole. It should have been reserved for England. For the richest, the deepest, and the loftiest shades of green in the world, we must go – to London. St James's Park, Hyde Park, Kensington Gardens, the innumerable Squares hold unbeatable grass, grass that takes the breath away... Pardon me! I'm trying to loosen the grip, but I haven't quite shaken off London yet. Its beauty even *as nature* is so compelling. Often I have come in from a home county in Spring or early Summer to find a greenery and floweriness that made the country seem grey. I cannot tell how often I have gone out of my way simply to pass through Lincoln's Inn Fields in order to see the dark, dark tree-trunks deeply rooted down upon that blooming green!

But to return. Shakespeare made one mistake. He should not have said *precious* stone. He should have said emerald stone. England's green and pleasant land – Blake's simple phrase has wedged itself into complete acceptance because it is the absolutely true description. When confronted with that green I find that even the bountiful resources of English prose are inadequate and I must employ the swifter and tighter rhythms of verse with which to celebrate the green fields of England:

> They slope, they curve, they swell,
> they rise in waves, they flow,
> they wash against the roads,
> they swirl around the single trees,
> they encompass cottages and farms,
> they island out the copses
> and beat against the woods –
> the green fields of England!
>
> The green fields of England –
> her secret and her sign,
> her word to all the world
> her heart, her song, her flag,
> her deepest truth divine.

If anyone doesn't see the justification for this enthusiasm let him walk through almost any county during March or April. Then the everlasting rich, green fields shine out almost as if illuminated from underneath. There is no greenery as yet upon the hedges or the trees, they are dark, they are nearly purple with the budding life. No other green interferes with the fresh spring-radiance of the fields. Seen from a knoll, the landscape spread below is that of a flashing, inspired, emerald isle. The English prefer to have uncultivated fields. They hate to dig a spade into the soil, and prefer to leave it alone, letting a few sheep and cattle graze on it. Hence the *quantity* wherever you go of untouched fields – flat, rounded, steep, sloping, curved, long, narrow, basined, square, triangular, every shape and sort.

3

That is my first impression of the countryside – the living green. And my second? No visitor can fail to be attracted by the potency of the Spirit of History that haunts this land. It is as ancient as it is modern. That which has been seems often more aerially intense than that which is. At one moment you are a contemporary of George VI: then turning off the motored high road you may suddenly become a contemporary of Caesar and Vercingetorix. At two p.m. you are at the very centre of modernity, in the vortex of its turmoil: an hour later you are standing in a village street belonging to the days of Queen Elizabeth, while the *existence* of what you have just come from can no longer be accepted by the mind. That is the experience which I have enjoyed most often in England: getting into a train with a ticket taking me back three hundred years or more.

We know all about the Celtic Twilight. But how about the English Twilight – or whatever you like to call it? It is as real a thing. I treasure the memory of my wanderings through that veil…

…My path lay uphill, and as I climbed, the slopes of Dorset spread out before me. A distant white road lay between two steep green fields and fell like a waterfall into a group of trees at the bottom from which a church tower rose.

The climb began to get easier and my path led me across a giant plate of grass. A lot of white-and-black stones were scattered on the green. When I approached they got up and flew away. They were peewits. They circled about restlessly with no objective. Their cries were borne across the ancient slopes in lament for something they for ever sought. Sad birds, they never sing, and are seen only in places where the spirit of Memory is stronger than the power of the everlasting Now.

I, a solitary pilgrim out in the windy loneliness of Time's leavings, looked down in front at the sea, and felt behind the enduring lawns stretch back like history-laden years.

Here is eternal England. This does not change. Great cliffs and mountains may change: but these gentle slopes, these long, low, green hills remain as they were. Thus it was at the dawning of the English day. Thus were they seen by the Roman legionaries and by those who came before the Romans – and before them. Thus shall they slant for ever.

Memories of Dorset! They are the memories that rise before me whenever I think of England, whenever I am tempted to doubt whether this old and beloved country can successfully withstand the invasion of the new barbarians from within.

I think of the Chesil Beach. I walk there again. To my left the sea; around me the hills and the horse-shoe; at my feet and far into the utterly deserted distance, the brown pebbles – an elementary theme. I look into the great winter waves which, as they pounce and fall, beat into my mind the divine message of incomprehensibility. I no longer walk with Caesar: I pace further back – even to the Fifth Day.

I take the steep track that rises up behind the village of Abbotsbury. As I mount, the houses seem to grow into a green-clasped hiding-place; the tithe barn sinks deeper into the soil and leans against a bank.

Soon I again descend into a vale cut between bulging green mounds and rondures which look almost as if they had been blown out with air from underneath. I descend into heaven. A citadel of trees, a lucid stream, one path: and in bond to these – a village. The trees stoop down upon the houses, the gardens line the stream. I have entered Utopia at last. Here a dream has been fulfilled. In this place Jerusalem has been established. Everything that has ever happened in the world is justified. I feel what Chekov felt when he listened to music, that all things are forgiven and that it would be strange not to forgive.

I mount again, and again I wander over the slopes and across the centuries that lie asleep. I reach Maiden Castle – or, rather the hill where the Fortress once stood. I climb over ring after ring of mounds which like dry, green moats encircle its site. On the summit is a blank waste of grass made blanker and still more lost by the sheep that graze in the wind. Not one stone of the Castle remains in sight – and yet its ghostly presence broods! Victim and inheritor of the present hour I wonder why I am straying on the ruins of an ancient day. With some relief I climb down again over the numerous amazing moats.[1]

A little further on and I come to another village. Another of the thousand villages of England, forgotten, lost, pocketed in Time. Many trees, four or five cottages, a pillar box and a church sum its count. It is Winterborne Came, once the parish of William Barnes, the poet who was a priest and the priest who was a poet. From here a closely tree-arched grassy drive, where the sun lights up a green that never shone before, leads to Thomas Hardy's final home… I approach the church and gaze up at its tower pencilled by the toil of Time – as I have gazed at hundreds in England, as I shall never cease to gaze with admiration and reverence and love whenever I see them, these hall-marks of the old English spirit, these imperishable pillars of tradition and pages of history! I pass beyond the church and look across a field at the

Big House. It is dying. Blinds are drawn over the windows – as if it had closed its eyes. The garden is untended. There is no movement any more.

I go on and find myself passing some great modern pylons striding across the land gigantically. They are the Present. But how strange! I seem to see them as *history*, as they will one day appear to others rather as Stonehenge appears to us now.

I reach a road, a Roman road, straight as a javelin, clean as a sword, which runs through Dorchester cleaving the town in two. In the evening I walk through the streets past the modern shops till, just outside, I come to a Roman amphitheatre. I climb down and walk about in the dark basin that holds the ancient hour. No one is there, of course.

No one could be there.

A few hundred yards away a fair is in full swing. The crowd gathers in the glaring lights, throws the balls, rides the horses, goes in the mechanical boats, while the blaring, screaming mechanical music drowns every other sound. The people are in this circle here. It would be impossible for any single one of them to break it and go to that other circle beyond – as impossible as to change their consciousness, as impossible as to go back a thousand years.

True mystic sight! The dark, empty arena given over to the ghosts of Rome: and only a few yards away in space but centuries away in time, the celebrants of the present generation confined in the circle of flame.

Next day I pass on making for Cerne Abbas. I walk now through the gentlest of all valleys, under the succour of diminutive hills, by the most quiet of all streams. Horses write their bodies on skylines. I approach a clump of trees: some cows appear to be grazing off its topmost leaves. Getting nearer I see that they are standing on the high green mound behind the clump.

Here is the reign of peace. The proud oppression, the waste place, the fearful cliff, the snowy gesture, the sweeping utterance in chasm and gorge and glacier by which Nature so often makes Man bow down before here, are lacking here. Fields deep with buttercups instead of snow, enduring slopes of green for the buttressed and brow-beating peaks, a calm stream for the raging river, smile upon me as I pass.

I reach Cerne Abbas – another village fallen into a sleep from which there is no waking. Someone drops a pail, and it can be heard over the whole village. Two women are gossiping, and their voices ring out in the still evening air.

Rounding a corner I come to the church. Its tower rises before me like a perpendicular hand raised in blessing. I go on into the churchyard and down a path cathedraled by trees and consecrated by aged stones, to a well – where holy water flows.

Why is history mighty and hallowed? Why are the ancient stones of the trodden ways sacred in our sight? Why do we not love the present until it has become the past? We shall know this only when we have unveiled the meaning of Time. All I know as I stand by the Well of Cerne is that I am in the presence of earth memories more powerful in the poetry of their haunting than the sad, grey prose of the present hour. This at my feet is the scripture of the abbots and the monks, and traced on the hill above is another writing by another age far earlier still, the figure of a giant whose gesture no man has dared to tamper with.

As the dusk descends I walk up on to the hills beyond the village. The dusk deepens, making the green slopes black and the grey road white. How different from some other times, I think, when the red maturing sky and darkened rills have divided earth from sky with sharply margined line. No clear panorama now; the path behind recedes into the gloom, and in front dissolves. The small hillock which in the bright light of another hour was but a knob graced with a valley's green, takes on the dimensions of a mountain, riding up into the misty air with no skyline to separate its summit from the endless ether.

England is not all a garden. Men still may go out to be lost in her solitude or tempted in her wilderness.

4

Monuments often if not always are symbols of how soon we forget rather than how long we remember celebrated men of action. Such has been my reflection many a time when passing over a certain hill in Dorset upon which there is a monument erected to Thomas Hardy – but not to that Hardy who needs no such monument.

Few can know or care much about the sailor and companion of Nelson. But the questioning soul and the burning heart of that other Hardy can never be forgotten, for his work is now part of the country's inheritance. In such things the English are very rich. Their Northern mountains are not something external to them, but have been interwoven with their culture and interpreted to their minds by the scribe of Rydal Mount. And all the Southern counties are vocal with the voice of this other bard. From Oxford to Land's End, from Weymouth to Ilfracombe, the words of this interpreter have thrown open the gates of compassion for the people, and have raised up Nature to the throne of God. It is true that Hardy externalized a God and cursed Him just as others externalized a God and praised Him. Those who praise Him do not always show any striking love for His works. But Hardy, the man who cursed the hour of birth and cried out with Job continually through the mouth of his characters: "Let them curse it that curse the day, who are ready to raise up their mourning. Let the stars of the twilight thereof be dark; let it look for light but have none; neither let it see the dawning of the day!" This man was fascinated by the earth. He may not have loved the Creator: he did love His creation. No man who hated Nature could have watched over her every movement, her every mood, with such care. No man who did not feel that underneath the catastrophe of life there yet bubbles up a lyric of everlasting praise for the fact of life, could have dwelt so magnificently upon the general spectacle and the minute particulars. In consequence his works do not have a logical effect upon the reader. We feel that though Jude has fallen he has not failed, and though Tess is given over to destruction she is not destroyed.

Thomas Hardy and Wordsworth are supreme examples of the English spirit. Their contact with Nature is direct, and never given up to *illegitimate* mysticism, to side-stepping into fanciful regions of fairydom – a danger to which purely Celtic writers have been exposed. Wordsworth pronounced many ultimate sentences from the exalted place: but no reader feels himself excluded from the possibility of a like vision; for Wordsworth did not leave the earth and wander off aerially, his feet were firmly on the unmisty soil, and he spoke of this world "which is the world of all of us, where we find our happiness or not at all." In Wordsworth we see the strength of true pantheism. There were no "Little Men" roaming the Wordsworthian hills. And though Hardy weaves spell upon spell over us by his power to summon up a positive Spirit of Nature, his world remains the solid earthly place we know.

5

To continue. It will be seen that the English village is a source of fascination to me. It is not surprising that this should be so to an Irishman. The Irish village is hardly a thing of beauty. A wide street with a row of white-washed hovels on each side would describe almost any of them in any county. When in England I often long to see them again – because of the people in them, the mountains never far away, the lucent air in which they are suspended. They *are* Ireland, somehow, and they seem to me more beautiful than official beauty. Nevertheless, the English villages have given me so much joy of another kind, so often, and in so many places, that my gratitude for them continually overflows.

I have mentioned four villages in a journey through the twilit slopes of Dorset. But if I were setting up as a guide it would not be in the South Country alone that I would propose to direct the steps of those who might follow me. I would not even insist that the Cotswolds are necessarily the most entrancing. I would say: Go anywhere, into any county almost, and do not omit the countryside within the industrial areas, for just as the Downs are celebrated for being anything but low, so the Black Country contains some of the prettiest parts of England, white in Spring and gold in Autumn, with even lovelier villages, churches, abbeys and manor houses than those in the Cotswolds – if that were possible (which it isn't). In these villages the traveller from another land halts, amazed; he experiences such a leafy calm and a peace so enchaining that it seems as if he had arrived at last in the harbour on the utmost shore. And the pleasure which these villages give to an Irishman is also due to the look of wealth and prosperity of the cottages – as compared with Ireland anyway. Each dwelling, well-built, clean, furnished (try the Irish cottage for furniture!); and each with a long strip of ground growing flowers and a large selection of rich, healthy vegetables.

The houses which do not suggest either health or wealth today are the old manor houses. The feeling of history in these places is extraordinarily intense, the beauty and the sadness enough to wring the dullest heart. Once this manor house was a vessel sparkling with purpose, a centre of activity radiating life around it. Now the purpose, the life, the meaning have fled, and only the hollow form remains, draped with the intolerable tapestries of memory and lament. Often the deep green grass is tended with loving care. The beds that line the ancient wall have been weeded. But the eyes of the great and lovely house are closed in mortal sickness. Every day the scene becomes more beautiful and every day it becomes more dead. Here we enter the gate of history. But we cannot close it behind us. That is why the melancholy of these halls is so immeasurable. We cannot close the gate. The feeling of transition is overpowering, the invasion of the Present not to be gainsaid.

These houses are in this state today owing to the sins of the fathers. The local communities of which they were the centre were swept away by a revolution. Not a revolution from below, but from above. Not a rising of the poor to rob the rich, but a rising of the rich to rob the poor. The Agricultural Revolution killed feudalism – though that was not the intended goal. There was a great deal to be said for feudalism. It meant that there was a considerable amount of communism. Not equality between all classes – far from it. But the common ownership of much land by *the many*. The least labourer possessed his strip of land: yet there was more common ground than private, and the labourer could supplement his wages not only by the fruits of his own strip, but throughout the year could gather fuel from the common wood and turf from the common moor, while the free meadows supplied pasture for his cow, and gleanings from the harvest supplied wheat for himself and beans for his pig.

The resultant social life is known, perhaps not wholly without significance, as Merry England. There seems to have been a certain happiness and independence of spirit. It was possible to rise and actually difficult to sink into beggary. There was room for idleness and inefficiency no less than for ambition and industry. It was possible for each locality to be a self-contained community, an organic, religious, social circle.

But when the machine arrived, expanding trade, bringing in labour-saving methods, creating factories, towns, communications, philosophical economists and an extra supply of babies, it became clear that if the rich were to become richer a more scientific method of agriculture was called for. And it was supplied. The feudalistic-communistic scheme was scrapped and Capitalism was born. It came rushing in destroying property until hardly anyone owned anything (today two-thirds of the population own scarcely more than a suit of clothes, and if anyone dares to insist that he *owns* his house or his garden or his car or his dog and will suffer no interference with regard to them, he is sent to prison). The commons were enclosed, railed off from the people, and within ten years, according to William Cobbett, laws, manners and characters changed out of recognition – and the old English peasantry was broken.

This Agrarian Revolution which changed England into an industrial nation was inevitable. The manner in which it was carried out was not inevitable but it was peculiarly English. There is seldom violence in England. When there is, it proceeds not from the under-dogs – who have always been somewhat abject – but from the over-dogs, who have always been somewhat truculent. (I would like to draw attention to this again later when mentioning the General Strike of 1926.) At the beginning of last century before democracy was born, this peculiarity was very marked. The September Massacres and guillotinings of the French Revolution (which saved the French peasant) do not stain the page of history so much as the massacres direct and indirect of this English Revolution (if by revolution we mean change, uprooting, slaughter, destruction and spoliation) which killed the English peasant. In the name of Efficiency, in the name of Public Spirit, in the name of the Nation's Prosperity more crimes were committed than in the name of Liberty. The new agricultural methods worked all right, they were a success; but the additional wealth went to the landlords, to the parsons, and to the big farmers. The peasants were disinherited. Machinery swallowed up their cottage industries. Wages, which had never been a sufficient support alone, went lower. Whole families lived on a shilling a day and were indirectly taxed sixpence a day. A regular system of small holdings would have been harmless and probably beneficial. But the revolutionaries desired it otherwise. They so far reduced the peasants that in many places they were treated as inferior horses, harnessed to carts and wagons, shut up in pounds made to hold stray cattle, put to work with bells round their necks with drivers set over them as if they were galley slaves, and sold for auction like furniture. When they became skeletons, systems of relief were introduced with such insincerity and brutality that the evils were only increased. But still there was no mercy. The one hope of a meal was to poach. This was made a criminal offence. In the game preserves of the rich, man-traps were laid in the undergrowth snapping with their crocodile teeth – and those who were caught in them were hanged or transported. At last they feebly tried to rebel with a little rick-burning and riots. The revolt was stamped out with the greatest of ease. Nine men were hanged, and amidst awful scenes of weeping relatives, four hundred and fifty-seven men and boys were transported to Van Diemen's Land and New South Wales under conditions so horrible that for those travellers there was but one hope, one prayer and one pleasure – the release of death.

Thus perished "the proud English peasantry" and the village Hampdens who "the petty tyrants of their fields withstood." It was the end of England as an agricultural nation – though no doubt agriculture itself was technically improved. But life went out of the country into the town, and that lack of life is still felt. And as democracy has gradually bettered the conditions of the labourer it has also exacted revenge upon the owners of the Big Houses. The manor house is no longer a pivot round which a local community gathers. The owners are stranded, and with little money, with no influence or significance or meaning in the life of the nation, they and their manors exist only as relics and anachronisms – or are sold to the uncultured rich.

6

Yet the slow death and neglect of these old manors strikes the traveller as very unnecessary. They ought to be the centres of new life in the new England of today. It seems so obvious. Here, all over the country are the most gracious and lovely halls and gardens, dying for lack of significance – empty vessels longing to be filled. Why should they not, wherever possible, be made into centres of local cultural activity? This may sound like an idle daydream. Yet it has been carried out in one such place already – at Dartington Hall in Devonshire. There, instead of the usual atmosphere of a lovely old ruin and demesne, belonging to history rather than the present day, you find a centre of activity, cultural and agricultural. It may be true that private individuals have run and financed this enterprise. But no one believes today that money cannot be found by the Government for any great enterprise that is thoroughly worth while. I cannot conceive of a happier circumstance for the owners of these old tottering houses than that they should find themselves financed to bring their decaying property to life and to be the pivots round which the new life of their neighbourhood would circle.

This is to say that these places should be made into the mental and spiritual and moral nurseries of the future – if England is to have a future. They should supply the need which is no longer supplied by the Church of England. They should be a dignified and delightful rallying point, the religious, the cultural and the idealistic centre of the local community.

The local community. The social circle. If one thing impresses me more than another about modern England, it is the lack of local communities and the lack of social circles.

This is partly explained by the mastery of the machine, which has brought about so much loneliness that we hear of more unhappiness and of suicides on this score than at any other time. On the surface this may seem strange. Owing to the machine life has become wider for everyone. Henceforth no man is limited by the village in which he lives. The skyline of the ploughed field is no longer the end of any man's vision. He has only to go to the nearest cinema to see far beyond that field. He need not go to the cinema, he need not stir from his house or cottage, for talkers, musicians and entertainers of all sorts are waiting on him if he will but turn the radio switch. And when he is bored with his particular place he has only to leap onto a bus, a tram, a train, a car, a liner, an aeroplane to be taken swiftly somewhere else.

But this unexampled advance in communication seems opposed to the profound desire for communion. There is only one thing people really want, and that is – congenial society. If we live in such a circle we can almost dispense with the motor car. If we like our neighbours we can almost do without the wireless. Yet never before in England has the neighbour been less liked. There is an unheard of amount of discussion on socialism and communism, but less social spirit and communistic spirit than ever before. There doesn't seem to be any society any more. In the old days people often groaned at the smallness and pettiness of their circle. Today nearly all circles have been broken down or blown up, and each person stands alone – or in a family unit (which is no longer a unity, for it cannot bear this strain). This is truer even of the town than of the country – though towns were built in order to bring people together. There never has been a greater loneliness than today.

It is interesting to note that a hundred years ago William Cobbett made the following entry during one of his rural rides, on Sunday evening, August 27th, 1826:

"I rode up to the garden wicket of a cottage, and asked the woman, who had two children, and who seemed to be about thirty years old, which was the way to Ludgarshall, which I knew could not be more than about *four miles* off. She did *not know*. A very neat, smart, and pretty woman; but she did not know the way to this rotten borough, which was, I was sure, only about four miles off! 'Well, my dear good woman,' said I, 'but you *have been* at Ludgarshall?' – 'No.' 'Nor at Andover?' (six miles another way). – 'No.' 'Nor at Marlborough?' (nine miles another way). – 'No.' 'Pray, were you born in this house?' – 'Yes.' 'And how far have you ever been from this house?' – 'Oh! I have been *up in the parish* and over *to Chute*.' That is to say, the utmost extent of her voyages had been about two and a half miles! Let no one laugh at her, and, above all others, let not me, who am convinced that the *facilities* which now exist of *moving human bodies from place to place* are amongst the *curses* of the country, the destroyers of industry, of morals, and, of course, of happiness."

This loneliness cannot be entirely explained by the advent of the machine. It is also the result of the decay of religious belief. Consider the words of T S Eliot in *The Rock*:

>What life have you if you have not life together?
>There is no life that is not in community,
>And no community not lived in praise of God...
>And now you live dispersed on ribbon roads,
>And no man knows or cares who is his neighbour
>Unless his neighbour makes too much disturbance,
>But all dash to and fro in motor cars,
>Familiar with the roads and settled nowhere.
>Nor does the family move about together,
>But every son would have his motor cycle,
>And daughters ride away on casual pillions.

It is not therefore surprising that the English people were told the other day that "religion is what men do with their solitariness" – a remark which was taken very seriously by the bishops since it was uttered by a scientist. The latter forgot to add that what men do after that solitariness is not unimportant – that only then does it become religion, a binding together of men in community. The Church of England no longer succeeds in creating communities. This is because it attempts to bring the people together on the basis of now controversial beliefs which have lost their vitality, and on the basis of morality: whereas if it were erected on the basis of *worship* of that which is beyond controversy, and on the basis of the *art of life*, then the Church could last for ever as a living and a leading force! This calls for clergy who are religious men instead of merely unartful moralists. But the student of England knows better than to ask for such a thing. He cannot hope for it. Yet how often have I hoped for it! How often have I yearned for the new priest when I have gazed upon the old vicarage gardens of England – those withered, fallen, lovely, perishing pools of peace. How often have I brooded upon this ideal when sitting alone in some village church still holding within its walls the silent message of the Divine. But I know that I must accept the declared and established fact of death – and that here, as always at last, a good thing must fall to the ground.

But it might not be impossible to turn the old manor houses into the new vessels of value. A church, a university, a school, a theatre, a social forum all rolled into one – that is the ideal. The born teacher, the born preacher, the born artist, the born moralist, the born talker, the men who are generally neglected and wasted today simply because they are original in their powers, would here find their haven and their work. Each place could be as different as it liked, according to the personalities of the directors and the vitality of the district.

There is a wonderful word in the English language called *nucleus*. Everyone who goes in for some freak thing says that he is forming a nucleus out of which will grow the new society. I am not much of a believer in these nuclei. One or two old manor houses carrying out the above ideal would not have much effect on the nation. But if a cultural campaign carried this out with the same thoroughness as the agricultural campaign for collective farming was carried out in Russia, then there might be a remarkable blossoming of social life in England, and of its neglected mental and spiritual life.

7

I love an old garden wall. My favourite piece of architecture is the great wall enclosing the Old Garden. Let me lean against that while the sun shines and I will surrender all else. I ask no more. Give me the moss-engrained, naturalized stone and the warm sun – give me that much, and the proudest spires, the loftiest cathedral aisles, the superb pavilions informed with prayer and praise will not so faithfully conduct me towards heaven. I would like to write an apostrophe or an ode to the walls of England. It is not strange that the English should possess the most inspiring walls. The desire to close the door, to be alone, to find seclusion, could not be more beautifully symbolized. The weak, silent Englishman may here fence in his easily bruised and alarmed soul from the affrighting world.

I lean against this ancient wall at Ightham Mote in Kent. Having paid my shilling and entered another era to wander through the dusty hours of long ago, to bathe in the adorable traditions of the mighty past, and to gaze down into the silent water of the moat through which swans, majestic as Royalty, glide in slow procession, I pass out again and walk over the gracious lawn, through the neglected garden, and under trees weighed down with splintered age. Then I come to the great garden wall and lean against it. No one looks from the window of the house. No gardener is in sight. I am the sole visitor from the twentieth century. There is a cold wind beyond, but none here, only the rays of the April sun. For a few minutes I am invaded by a peace that passes comprehension, such as others have obtained through the purity of their natures or the tension of their souls. For I have entered into a quiet place where no evil is, where protection from the barbarity and malice of the progressing world is granted, and I am at one with the blazing globe above.

Thus having entered the gate of history I *have* closed it behind me. And I am inclined to say that after all perhaps if these little kingdoms can do this for us, why should they do more, and how could they do more?

This castle of indolence and slow time is in Kent. It is a curious fact, but geographical distance from London is by no means a sure test of distance in atmosphere. There are many places in Kent further away in this sense than Devonshire, little dales almost as savagely unmodern as some glens in County Wicklow – places where tradesmen hardly penetrate and where no workman will go and do a job. There are staggeringly beautiful villages like Chiddingstone so utterly Shakespearean that no one staying there could possibly think of Freud. And there is no county in which the eternal verities of English loveliness are more richly displayed. In the woods of Kent the holy living and holy dying of uncontaminated wild nature, from the rising up of the year to its casting down, are unbeatable. Its bluebell revelations in May, when the sky seems positively to have been laid upon the ground, make one re-examine philosophies and look out upon the world with fresh eyes.

Yet in the middle of this, and a few yards as it were from Ightham Mote, the Machine Age displays itself with more concentrated magnificence than perhaps anywhere else in England. If you want to see the essence of modernity it is only necessary to look down on the Maidstone Road on a summer Sunday evening.

One such evening I turned off a lane onto this highway. I wanted to cross over, but could not do so. It had become a ferocious river of light. I was on an eminence and could see its course for some distance. It was an unceasing chase of motor cars with not one going from the direction of London – as well might a bit of water try to run back against a stream. I wanted to cross over and drive against it for a mile. But no – I stood on the edge of the twentieth century roaring past and ready to crush me if I opposed its flow for a second.

The chariot races of an earlier era could not have presented a finer spectacle. And I noticed how if anyone fell off one of the cars or was crushed to death by getting in the way, the people concerned would always stop to pick up the fallen man or corpse, and the dead or dying were always cared for and ministered to by the drivers themselves (nevertheless the mastery is so great that there are said to be scarcely more than a few thousand casualties in a year). Each era presents its own spectacle. This highway, I reflected, on a fine summer evening is a pinnacle of art, one of the great triumphs of Man, fleeting witness to the skill of his hand, the flashing of his mind, and the tenderness of his heart.

I am all for enjoying the present contribution however much I may also love to contemplate the past contribution, but to those in England – and they are many – who hate the Machine Age and see in it the perishing of all that they hold most dear, I would say: Calm yourselves. Be of good cheer. It will pass. Everything passes. We know that joy and goodness never remain long by our side. Neither does sorrow nor the bad thing. The Machine Age will eventually pass away. The machines will not be suddenly destroyed by angry men – that is only one of the fancies of Samuel Butler. They will die out. People will lose the taste for them. We cannot conceive such a thing at present. But tastes do come and go in the strangest way. From the earliest times it was obvious to anyone who observed a boiling kettle, that there was great power to be got out of steam. But the taste for using such power did not occur until the nineteenth century. The compass was discovered by the

Chinese long before Europe discovered it – but they felt no desire to navigate the world. They discovered gunpowder, but they merely used it for fireworks, being lamentably lacking in the taste for blowing themselves to pieces with it. The taste for machinery will die out, inexplicably. So let us rejoice in the spectacle while it is before our eyes, and salute the inexhaustible energy which Blake said was eternal delight.

And if my words fail to produce the necessary calm, I would say: Come with me to a certain spot on this Maidstone Road, and I will demonstrate to you the ordained and ultimate triumph of Nature.

This spot I speak of is the site of a garage, and the open space round the garage. The ground of this clearing is not made of soil. Bolts, screws, nails, nuts, broken bits from tools, meet the eye; look closer and still no earth can be seen – only tiny screws and nails, miniature nuts, pieces of metal, washers, ends of wire all crushed together into a smooth dark surface.

Part of this area is filled by a garage in the middle, backed by a variety of sheds. Two bungalows crouch down on each side, as if born diseased and blighted. The space between each bungalow and the garage is heaped with the wreckage of machinery. The nose of a Morris Cowley wipes the dust; the chassis of another sits upon the ground open to the sky; inextricable tangles of wire and degutted engine defeat the endeavour of two sides and four wheels to suggest a living car; the back of a saloon sits wheelless on the ground; old tyres lie about; half a hood shields a back axle; three or four outwardly whole cars, now for ever stationary, wedged in dying embrace and clothed snow-deep in rust, provide one bungalow's barrier against the east wind.

The inhabitants of the bungalows are a queer lot – the men of machines, the new species. They are happy enough, being very creative. They take a car, hack it to bits, tear out its engine, its carburettor, its battery, its magneto, its half-shafts, its bearings, its steering-wheel, its tyres: they seize another for repair, and push and pull and grip and peer until it lives again. The hours pass. They lose all sense of time under their energy of creation. They, the modern race, a species that could never have been prophesied, are very different in appearance from the men of horses who came before. Their faces are not weather-worn nor tanned nor elementarily sage; their hands are not dirty with the dust of the earth, but thickly grimed with every sort of oily darkness; their eyes never look upward into the sky, nor across any field. The derelict scene around is to them a sight of flowers, a garden, and a lawn.

Yet the same group never seems to stay in this place long. They remain for six months or so and then fade out. For another six months the place may be empty. It is worth a special visit during these vacant periods.

I remember once going there on one of these occasions hoping to see one of the mechanics. He had disappeared. I walked round the premises. The inhabitants of both bungalows had gone. All was silently desolate. I had been inside one of the bungalows – a scene more chaotic than outside, more extraordinary indeed in the dilapidation of the furniture and annihilation of comfort, than something in a dream. On this occasion I stood outside the other one. The scene held my attention. The half-broken windows were filled in with rags, the top of the door patched like a pair of trousers – the whole smudged with disease and early death. Two pails full of rubbish stood immediately outside the door; there was a tea-pot on the ground beside a ruined kettle; a few yards out, all by itself, a water-cock rose from the earth like an erect snake; old tyres, piles of machinery entanglement, bonnets of cars, pieces of rubber, wrecked hoods, lay around.

They commanded attention. But what held me more was the triumph of Nature and of Time over all this. Everything here was *temporary* save mother earth and father time. Marvellous to observe how the hard unbending iron was melting into powder under the motion of the air! The strong machinery was sinking into the earth whence it came. The hulking vessels were being overthrown by the movement of a root, by the pressure of a leaf. Steadily and without pause the slender green shoots were quietly covering the unresistant metal. It would not be long before the same strange power of gentleness had removed the bungalows from mortal sight.

So, in this graveyard of mechanism, I attended at the resurrection of everlasting life.

---

1 The Excavations of today have now altered this site remarkably.

PART TWO

3

A UNITED PEOPLE

"Make no mistake about it, the English have organization," said John Kettle to Dr Oliver Gogarty. They have. They have organization. But it is not superimposed from above, military-wise. It is a spontaneous working together – an almost chemically organic process of units in a unity.

This is because England of all countries in the world is most a *nation*. There is no question of her having to insist that she is a nation or that she ought to be or shall be or has been: she simply happens to be a nation more than others; and therefore less than others does she have to think about this status. That's what Irishmen in England find so attractive: the fact that there is no need for the people to think of England as an Old Woman for whom one should die or, better, cause someone else to die. In Ireland, patriotism does not bring out the collective virtues so much as the individual vices: it is often a question of a bitter personal flame to which, under the cloak of some pitiable phrase, may be sacrificed the lives of other Irishmen. In Italy we see it taking the form of national exhibitionism, an insistence that they the Italians (actually a nation of children) are very important people and are, indeed, Romans led by a Caesar who also combines the attributes of a Napoleon – for does he not stand before them with one arm upraised like an ancient senator while the other is thrust into the breast of his jacket like the

Man of Destiny? In Germany an intense militant patriotism is the answer to a humiliating treaty.

Owing to the happy circumstances of her geography and her history, English nationalism contrasts favourably with others. It is what it ought to be – a consciousness of nationhood. People continually refer to "the Nation," which is conceived not as an aggressive or an assertive body over against others, but as their very own private thing, as themselves. Treasures, parks, museums, estates are constantly "given to the nation." The English regard it as self-evident that they are a unity, and it would never occur to them to get this "recognized" from outside. When their unity seems threatened from without or within they rise to the occasion and organize themselves in a solid body "for the sake of the nation." No strong man is called upon to weld the people together. This is a great advantage – for welding from above impoverishes the rich nature of a country. As it must be done by force, we see in Germany the Prussian element trampling down the Bavarians, the non-military men whose contribution to the world's culture is not small. But the English people are so much of a unity that parliamentary government has always been their best method of advance.

However much they may divide themselves up into conservatives, liberals or socialists, they all regard themselves as part of one machine whose object is to progress. The thing is always seen as a *whole* car: one party the engine, another the brakes – all oiling it with goodwill. One takes risks, the other cautions. One outrages conscience, the other salves it: Conservatives add to the Empire, Liberals denounce them for doing so, and conscience thus laid to rest they can jointly apply Liberal cement. This unbounded sense of the whole, the nation, is often called the special English "state sense." It is very un-Marxian. The tussle between the Government Benches and the Opposition is carried out almost in the spirit of a football match with the Speaker as referee, and the side which sustains most injury regards the matter in a sporting light, saying: "Ah, well, I suppose it's all part of the game." It is felt that (as in a game) two sides are necessary if a satisfactory goal is to be reached (or kicked). Bonar Law (was it a pseudonym?) stands up for two hours to a steady fire of interruption about unemployment from the Northern Members. Afterwards he says to them: "You Clyde boys were pretty hard on me today. But it's fine to hear your Glasgow accent. It's like a sniff of the air of Scotland in the musty atmosphere of this place." And immediately his attackers are made to feel that "though differences of opinion there may be" they are all really aiming at the same thing. They like to use the terms conservative, liberal, labour, but when it is thought expedient to drop the fiction that one of these parties is more progressive or more capable than the other, they do so and pool their mental resources. Thus in 1931 when Ramsay MacDonald was Prime Minister he soon found that a Labour government could not carry on a capitalist system without the help of the able capitalists in the House. Realizing that the nation might come to grief if he did try and carry on as he was, he formed a non-Party, a National Government, and presently handed the reins to Baldwin again. That solution to a crisis provided a good example of the British method. It was therefore applauded by the nation at large, though it was considered open to criticism by those who were of the opinion that a Labour government should smash instead of carry on the capitalist system.

This state-sense dovetails with their practical sense as against the theory and the doctrine. Their concern is always to "see results," to progress. In theory it is best to do this with a plan. In practice it is found better not to have a plan but to advance on the steps of opportunity. Opportunism is the only method open to a people who dislike thinking their way but are extremely good at feeling their way. The English are so good at it in fact that when they stop to reflect upon their course they gibe at themselves and say, "muddling through as usual!" There are other nations who often wish that they possessed the extra faculty with which to do this.

This is the famous English lack of logicality. It is a sort of political mysticism, a belief not only in the fluid quality of life, but a faith that all will work out for the best if they drift with the winding river of life. Hence consistency is regarded as unnatural. First principles are seen as dangerous rocks. A plan which threatens to work on a large scale has always been regarded with the gravest suspicion. Hence, when after the Great Fire Wren drew up a thorough plan for the rebuilding of London, it was inevitably turned down. Thus the roads in the country and the streets in the capital approach their objective with the same uncertainty as the politicians approach theirs.

Nevertheless it has often been granted – not least by such profound students of England as Renier and Max Beer – that the English are a highly revolutionary, progressive and pioneering race. They bring about revolutions without Revolution. They are able to do this because their conservatives are also progressive. Rather than let the power slip from their hands the capitalists re-form the existing forms. Often, of course, they won't do this till the last moment, but they do do it before it is too late. So far that has been the history of social advance in England – socialistic measures carried through by conservatives. A hundred years ago, owing to the suddenness of the Industrial Revolution, the condition of the workers was worse – if my reading of nineteenth-century history is correct – than it has ever been anywhere at any time. Consequently all parties for the last hundred years have steadily addressed themselves to the amelioration of those conditions. The results of this evolutionary revolutionism is that the changes for the better have been so great that the average worker today does not desire to risk achieving the further necessary reforms by unconstitutional means. His low wages – not low in comparison with the last century's wages, but low nevertheless, for however you look at it labour is absurdly paid considering its importance and its general unpleasantness – are supplemented by the State in so many different ways through health insurance, education and flat rents that his economic problem does not weigh upon him as heavily as upon the hosts of people in the class just above him. His parliamentary representatives, even Clydeside Members, declare that the changes for the better in recent years are so great as to make capitalism approximate closer and closer to socialism (indeed socialism and capitalism hardly seem to be regarded today in England as absolute antitheses: not long ago it was possible to point at some leader and say: "He's a socialist, but he owns a motor car!"; while today such a remark would sound as silly as saying in a low voice: "I'm afraid he's married an actress!"). His immense trade-union powers, while giving him a comfortable feeling that he is standing up for his rights, at the same time relieve him of responsibility: he will do what his leaders tell him, and they, of course, have little interest in red revolution. Thus trade-unionism is a powerful curb on either too much socialism or too much capitalism.

Hence gradualism succeeds in England. It suits the English people. But this does not mean that the forward movement is steady in its gradualness. Advances are made by short rushes and occasionally by big jumps. At the present time a very big jump, a leap forward into perhaps a new era in the history of mankind, is called for. And this is realized. The problem of how to distribute the abundance caused by the material success of industrialism, of how to give out purchasing power, is recognized everywhere as *the* modern problem. I have little doubt that the country which pioneered into industrialism will produce (has in fact already produced) the new pioneer who can show the way to make the success of machinery a still greater success instead of a tragedy. The problem of unemployment has reached such proportions that the gradual progress achieved for the working man has been lost in whole industrial counties.[1] But if matters only get critical enough in England they are always tackled at last with proper zeal. Another big jump forward is now due. Not in the name of socialism so much as in the name of social credit. The Government has already taken the step of paying out handsome wages to those engaged in making not-goods –

armaments. Ministers are bound to recognize that, from an economic point of view, they might as well hand the money, the purchasing power, straight across without demanding the not-goods. But it is a first step. The New Economists call it social credit and do not demand that the money shall come out of the taxpayer's pocket or that the receiver of the money shall produce a gun in exchange. As this credit movement in England is open to immediate practice and to partial experiment and does not call upon anyone to swallow a theory of Complete Change overnight or to take a nineteenth-century economist as a modern prophet, its future is not without promise.

Of course everyone in England does not take this view. Many of the most vital enthusiasts today do not seem to understand what can and what cannot be done in this country. The extremely vigorous Left Movement abhors the idea of gradualism, whether by jumps or not. Rather than address itself to the great specific wrongs and injustices and wedge in the experimental axe by constitutional means, it holds to the theory of total revolution. Such a movement is profitable in so far as it creates an atmosphere in which something has to be done. Nevertheless, the more detached observer cannot help feeling that much of the finest progressive energy is now wasted in England on theoretical squabbling, men who are really on the same side fighting each other instead of demanding and getting specific wrongs righted. No one can fail to be impressed by the tenderness of the social conscience in England today. In the last century the poor, as Chesterton pointed out, were forgotten. No fear of that now. The only thing that seems to me to hold up specific reforms on a huge scale is the threat of revolution and communism. Such threats provoke all the impulses of fear and resistance amongst the powers that be. Something much more cunning than this is needed.

The man who wants a revolution in this country is unable to call upon an army of enraged workers – and without this he might as well shut up shop. What one does see from time to time is the pathetic and totally unwarlike Hunger Marchers. Not long ago, standing on an improvised erection at the Marble Arch, I wondered whether what I witnessed was not the strangest spectacle in the social history of England since the Chartists marched into Westminster with their roll of signatures five miles long.

On my right was the Regal Cinema. Two immense cardboard pictures depicted the lineaments of George Arliss fixed in amused quizzical gaze. By a coincidence that seemed almost occult he was taking the part, according to the placard, of THE WORLD'S GREATEST FINANCIER. By chance or by mystic law, here was the perfect symbol placed at the corner of the Edgware Road. For, looking towards that corner I watched a host of Hunger Marchers advance into the Park. A thick river of men, accompanied protectively by an enormous number of policemen, rounded that corner. It flowed on for over an hour. Would it ever stop? Continuous cheers rose from the watching crowd, and from some of the marchers themselves. Those cheers, though not as impressive as a profound silence would have been, made the scene more poignant – for what had cheering to do with this? I climbed down from my view-point and joined the hundred thousand in the Park. It was not with a hundred thousand soldiers that I mingled. I was in the company of men who were doomed to live without routine, without purpose, without order, without enough to eat. Few of them bothered to listen to the speakers ranged four deep on a number of platforms... I looked beyond the massed Marchers to the top of the Marble Arch – the gateway leading to nowhere – on which the Commissioner of Police was "directing operations"; and I thought it doubtful whether Xerxes, who was wont to mount a hill to watch the proceedings of his hosts, could have beheld anything more remarkable. And I turned my eyes to the left where the face of THE WORLD'S GREATEST FINANCIER overlooked the scene – with perfect congruity.

And I thought – and still think – that all this nonsense will soon pass away, and that its passing will be "through constitutional means" brought about by the entrenched powers, before it is too late. The fact, which no emphasis can over-emphasize, is that in England almost anything can be done so long as it is done "constitutionally." Keep the old forms, and do what must be done – no matter how revolutionary or experimental – by dignified and orderly means through parliamentary procedure and the machinery of government. It is because the English understand the secret of being traditionalists and revolutionaries at the same time, that they may yet bring about changes more sweeping than the Bolshevists themselves. Their very love for old forms and hallowed names and ritualistic procedures gives them the power to preserve the continuity of the social structure no matter how much they alter it. The Mace lying across the treasury box in the House has a sobering effect upon Honourable Members. To the stranger it may look queer lying there. Two hundred and eighty-four years ago Cromwell asked: "What shall we do with this bauble?" and said, "Take it away." But as it was not a bauble but a concrete chunk of the English character, it soon was put back again. And there it is likely to remain, a symbol of the English continuity of tradition no matter what measures may be taken, a surety that a violent break with the past will be opposed by the majority of the people. The wig of the Speaker strikes the visitor as strange. But it also is a real expression of the desire that legality shall preside over the affairs of the nation. It would do equally well if he were dressed in the robes of a priest, for he is morality as well as legality, he is the spirit of religion as the English understand it. Hence when an Honourable Member walks out of the House he turns at the door, and though he does not cross himself, he bows to the Chair as if it were an altar.

Indeed, no student of England should underestimate the influence of the Law upon the people. "I'll have the law on yer!" is a phrase heard more often than any other. "Good Lord! don't you know it's *illegal!*" one man will say to another in a scared voice concerning some proceeding which in the eyes of God looks innocent enough. Hearing these words the other will immediately desist, knowing that what he is doing is wrong. Hence in 1926, when Sir John Simon declared the General Strike to be illegal, the nation knew it was wrong and acted accordingly; and when quite recently the same lawyer reminded the House of Commons that "Prime Minister" is a term "unknown to the Law," everyone felt confident that inasmuch as the head of the Government cannot properly be said to exist, England is safeguarded against ever having a dictator.

2

How does a violent revolution start? It starts as a rebellion. What is a rebellion? It is a mutiny. And a mutiny occurs when the human self-respect and the reasonable ease and comfort of workers are threatened by ruthless inhuman exploiters. The French and Russian aristocracy were foolish enough to provoke a mutiny and thus give the *philosophes* and the Marxists the opportunity to connect first principles with the electricity of anger. Between 1790 and 1830 England stood in great danger of being involved in similar events owing to the behaviour of their own almost equally ruthless and cruel aristocracy, but she was saved from this by the tremendous force of a conservative-rebel, a typical Englishman in the large – William Cobbett. Any violence there was came from above, not from below. I believe that the same holds true today. Violence is not inconceivable in England – from above. Either constitutional progress or violence from above – that is still the alternative.

Once I was standing in Piccadilly at the Hyde Park end opposite one of the big clubs there. I was watching yet another Hunger March demonstration which was going past. On the balcony of the club were two men. One of them stood looking down on the marchers below, unmoving as a rock, calm, sad, thoughtful, brave. There was a great reserve of power in that figure. I see him still. I also see the man who stood next him on the balcony. He also was English, but he was not calm. His body was twisting about in the most extraordinary way as he watched the Red Flag go past. His face was twitching continually. He was opening and shutting his fists, and talking into the air – for the other man took no notice of him. But I saw somehow very clearly that neither of these men would ever surrender his position to the masses without a terrific fight. And one of them at least would not hesitate to shoot.

In certain quarters there is even a desire to fight if the opportunity presents itself. This was illustrated by the events during the General Strike of 1926. I was present in London at the time, and the whole thing struck me as a particularly English affair, from start to finish. Owing to the severe slump preceding 1926 the "owners" of the coal mines had decided to reduce the wages and lengthen the hours of the miners – without making any appreciable sacrifices themselves. The miners refused to stand for this. They were backed up by the other trade-unions, railwaymen, engineers, transport workers, printers and so on, and they all struck together – though it must be remembered that the word "strike" has been changed to suit the spirit of the people, and means "not work."

They all struck together. But they gave the impression that they were just "trying it on" to see what would happen. They were apologetic. They assured the people that there was nothing revolutionary in what they were doing, that it was all perfectly legal (with which last point Sir John Simon did not agree!). They guaranteed that there would be no stoppage of food supplies. They suppressed their own papers – with the result that the one audible voice telling the nation what was happening came from Winston Churchill who managed to run a paper called *The British Gazette*. The busmen allowed non-strikers, university men in plus-fours, to take over their vehicles – one of the bus-drivers even going so far, it is told, as to give driving lessons to the Oxford undergraduate who was in possession of his automobile.

In this atmosphere the large public in England, which never seems to belong to either "the workers" or "the governing classes," went about its business with its usual complete ignorance of what was going on, and with its world-famous calm. Mr Smith, at his accustomed hour in the morning, closed the hall-door of 34 Laburnum Avenue, took three steps, opened his garden gate, shut it, and walked on to the main road. Instead of catching the 9.15 electric train to Charing Cross, he stood on the road, observed what cars were approaching, and then selecting the one he liked the look of best, he held up his hand. It immediately stopped, took him up and drove him to town, the occupants speaking quietly the while on the gravity of the situation. Later in the day he bought a half-sheet (many papers got out a half-sheet) in which he would find himself described as "courageous, calm, sensible, and confident."

The streets of London resembled a sort of Sunday, though slightly less so. More like a Sunday than a revolution. The man-in-the-street walked about, gaping. Sometimes people gathered in twos and threes, sometimes in crowds. It was considered good fun, this hold-up of everything. London life is so dull, so much the same thing day after day, that Londoners tremendously enjoy a bit of drama and the chance to display their individuality and good temper. They talked to each other even without an introduction. They mutually displayed their ignorance of the issue which had brought about the Strike. I occasionally asked someone whether he did not think that the miners were in the right. But I soon gave it up, for such a question caused visible embarrassment. If I said to someone: "I suppose it's all due to the boom in coal-prices after the War, for even after the Sankey Report coal stood at £4 a ton. Now that the slump has come it is less than £2 a ton. Hence reduction in wages. Hence even a Coal Subsidy. But since the owners aren't making much sacrifice, does anyone blame Cook for being so vocal in his slogan of 'Not a penny off the pay, not a second on the day'?" – I was not popular. I uttered some such words to a man in a group of people who had gathered to watch an amateur bus-driver trying to deal with a break-down. But my man backed away from me with a "I dunno; looks to me like there ain't no fair play somewhere." The words "price," "boom," "slump," "Sankey Report" and "subsidy" were hateful to him. I could see that he heartily wished that there weren't such things, and that everyone would be fair to everyone else, and leave him alone, and not make life feel so insecure.

The average Englishman loathes politics and general affairs. I am interested to see that that is also the finding of H G Wells. If anyone ought to know he ought – the great H G Wells. Let me salute him as I pass: a great man, a giant, a wonderful decoration to England of which he is amazingly representative, the very soul of England, for ever aspiring, hoping for the best, believing in the good. Some deny him greatness with a big G – as if there were not many kinds of literary greatness! He does not scale the high peak – true. But think what he does do. He is the historian of half a contemporary century, reliable, significant, embracing. His works cannot perish, for they mirror the living people, the times, the thoughts, the failings, the ideas and the ideals of a whole generation. The liveliness and the skill with which he does it should well make any detractor pause: the man is incredibly talented, and in his own way a giant. And he knows the English people, he knows what he's talking about, and I for one humbly support his remark – "The common man wants to do nothing with general affairs – wants to be left alone. Why not leave him alone?"

As for the specific working men in this business, they disliked the idea of violence. That is generally realized. It is not realized that though violence is disliked in the quarter from which it usually comes, it is not frowned upon by a section of the governing classes. In spite of the fact that the Prince of Wales personally contributed to the miners' Relief Fund, and in spite of the fact that the miners and the police played football together at loose moments during the Strike, there was a powerful section of men who, nominally in the cause of national unity, were determined "to put the working man in his place" and keep themselves in their place. This section, which always exists in England, is powerful, and at the time of the General Strike was represented by Winston Churchill, a man of splendid parts, one of which parts is a love of battle (it is reported by someone who sat behind him in a theatre during a war-play that he bristled with excitement and delight during the fighting scenes). This Minister and some of his immediate colleagues were all for a show of violence during the Strike. On the third day I met a long procession of armoured cars and tanks going through the streets. It was a disquieting spectacle. The excuse was to protect vans of foodstuffs, in spite of the fact that there was no one in England who had the slightest intention of touching them. The Government paper, the *British Gazette*, insisted that "the whole social order has been struck at, and must be defended." Bolshevism, it made clear, had at last raised its red hand. Quantities of policemen and soldiers were posted all over the place as if waiting for a September Massacre. A large number of Special Constables were sworn in who walked in the streets with armlets and truncheons. Opinion was suppressed through Broadcasting. And finally a proclamation was issued to the Army making it clear that violence, if it proved necessary, would be condoned and exonerated: "All Ranks of the Armed Forces of the Crown are notified that any Action they may find it necessary to take in an Honest Endeavour to aid the Civil Power will receive both Now and Afterwards the full support of the Government."

The strikers quailed and lost confidence. They talked about doing the thing thoroughly – stopping all letters, telegrams, gas, electric light and food. The real power was in their hands, and only the appearance of power in the hands of their opponents. They did not use it. They did not want that kind of revolution. They surrendered without even coming to terms with the owners. The Strike ended abruptly, and the public was informed that a great victory had been achieved over Bolshevism – in token of which the guards of the Southern Railway were made to replace their red ties with blue ones.

In this extremely English affair we should not fail to observe three things: the mildness of the under-dogs, the potential ferocity of the over-dogs, and the calmness of the general public. It was proved again that the English are endowed with the instinct of quiet co-operation in the highest possible degree. The nation at large even took this serious challenge to supersede Parliament, in a spirit of fun. "People laughed at each others' difficulties and at their own," says David Kirkwood. "When I saw car loads of girls driving through the streets of London looking upon the experience as if it were a picnic, I knew that we were beaten."

3

We have been continually told that the War made the world unsafe for democracy and unfit for anyone except heroes to live in. There is truth in this. Nevertheless democracy in England retains a certain reality.

It is easy to show that the people of England are not really free – though why perfect freedom should ever be thought desirable, and why it should be considered synonymous with democracy, are other questions. But a formidable list of their chains and of the petty persecutions to which they are subjected could be drawn up. The stringency of the *inaudible* censorship in high places which goes unnoticed owing to the very loudness of the prating about free news, free views, and free speech generally, is something which would make the average citizen gasp – but he knows little of the things which are suppressed with the velvet glove. Possibly only the long-suffering English would put up with the pettiness of the kind of law which forbids a workman to deliver two kinds of goods in the same van. It is extremely doubtful whether any other nation on earth harbours so many busybodies who actually have the power to prevent the public hearing or seeing anything which might ruffle and broaden their political, religious or moral ideas. The words liberty and freedom, always impossible to regard as concrete absolutes, melt under too close a scrutiny in England as much as in any other country.

Yet democracy does not do badly in England. To a large extent the people are represented in Parliament, whereas only a little more than a hundred years ago Members were frequently sent to the House from constituencies which did not exist – Old Sarum was a mound, Dunwich was under the sea. It was then a criminal offence to knock an MP's hat off. Honourable Members and the hats of Honourable Members are held in less reverence today, for they are responsible to the people who vote for them, and what they say in Westminster is reported – though not in the popular papers because editors realize that the people don't really want to hear about it. As a general rule the Ministers govern the people rather than are governed by them, but the

English populace possesses a voice which can sometimes be heard, which when heard is obeyed by those above. On occasion they can and do dictate their pleasure, they can and do refuse to be dictated to by politicians or Press lords. In politics the English are not schoolchildren, and they refuse to take down any dictation. They would rather be badly governed by a man who did not presume to dictate to them than well governed by one who did (Cromwell was careful to call himself a Protector).

Thus it sometimes happens that the voice rising from the street is more powerful than the will of the Government. As a rule, however, this national voice is only heard on questions of foreign policy, for that is the only thing about which the people in a body really feel strongly. The sufferings of some animals and foreigners move them more actively than the sufferings of their distressed countrymen; and when their own rulers have been responsible for some foreign victimization, they turn them, slowly perhaps but steadily, from that course. The majority of the English people have never wanted to injure the Irish in any way, and the Irish know it.

The most recent and the most dramatically rounded-off illustration of the voice of the people making itself effective was provided by the affliction of Abyssinia. Hardly anyone in England could say offhand where Abyssinia was or really knew what the thing was about. An injustice was sensed – and that is all. Personally, I'm not clear as to the rights and wrongs of that affair either, but I believe it was an injustice because the English people felt it to be such.

Their action was typical, beautifully expressive of their permanent but unthorough and unfanatical idealism. The Italians must not be allowed to do this. The statesmen knew that such was the feeling of the country. What could they do but be as vocal as possible against the injustice in spite of the fact that mere sincere vocal complaint can cut no ice with those who are not idealists. Mussolini, who is not an idealist any more than others on the Continent, took no notice. He knew the English well enough to count upon merely endless idealistic talk carried on with a real belief that everything would come to an amiable and idealistic issue. He himself insincerely threw them some promises at intervals. At last Sir Samuel Hoare, the Foreign Secretary, realizing that no progress was being made and at the same time considering that British idealism should not be fanatical and lead to war, attempted with the help of French diplomacy to rescue Abyssinia from complete destruction before it was too late. He actually succeeded in doing this, but immediately had to undo it because of the Voice of the People. They refused to stand for it. Far better, they declared, that the Abyssinians should be absolutely destroyed than that the English should countenance a deal with Mussolini, renounce the Ideal, and be privy to the signature of

Injustice. The Press took a less exalted view, but had no influence on the people. They would not allow it. Bowing to their will, Sir Samuel Hoare rose in the House of Commons to scrap his attempted treaty and to tender his resignation as one no longer worthy to serve the country. He made a brief speech, one of the most interestingly English ever uttered, something even approaching the sublime. A short time previously he had said to the people over the air from Geneva: "I have tried to say what is in your minds" – words uttered with a slow, clear deliberation a thousand times more eloquent than the gaudiest libertarian purple patch would have been. Now he rose in the House after having thought it best to adopt another policy. He rose – a strong, cold, clear, unemotional Englishman. He said, while tendering his resignation, that he naturally stood by his action as being the only wise one in the circumstances. But the people were not behind him, he went on, he had lost the confidence of the people. And as he said this his voice faltered and tears came into his eyes. He did not wipe them away. He spoke on standing upright and firm. It was clear to all who heard him that he was suffering deeply at the thought that he no longer held the confidence of the people, and as the Members looked at him they too felt that indeed there could be no deeper grief.

Such a scene must for ever dispose of the fiction that the English are cunning and hypocritical. They don't know the meaning of the words! In this country one quality is worshipped above all others – sincerity. Insincerity is the only unforgivable sin – worse than unchastity. "He is sincere anyway" – how many times we hear that remark in England. The amount of things that are committed and forgiven in the name of sincerity in all departments of the national life would make a remarkably varied list. And this people of all people on earth, feels continually drawn towards international affairs, for ever meddling with leaders and nations who are seldom sincere. No wonder their good intentions often make matters worse. No wonder they are always getting their fingers burnt. No wonder Continental observers like the brilliantly searching Professor Renier feel their hearts bleed for "the poor, weak, exploited English, always the under-dog, always the deceived party, always the cat's-paw of scheming adventurers."

4

Yet we cannot think of England in terms of an island only. She would be of no more importance in the affairs of the world than other small countries if it were not for her league of nations, often called the British Empire. They say that it contains within it the seeds of a greater league of nations dedicated to world peace. I don't quite follow why it contains this germ – and I must leave it to politicians to carry the discussion further. But while writing about England, I do not forget the existence of the British Empire. It is so expressive of the people. Indeed, when I think of their history the same image always comes before my mind, I see England as a net cast into the water off the coast of Europe, catching within its coils the wilder natures who fled the mainland. I think of the words written by Havelock Ellis, himself the son of a sea-captain: "What a strange fate it is that made England! A little ledge of beautiful land in the ocean, to draw and to keep all the men in Europe who had the sea in their hearts and the wind in their brains, daring children of Nature, greedy enough and romantic enough to trust their fortunes to waves and to gales. The most eccentric of peoples, all the world says, and the most acquisitive, made to be pirates and made to be poets, a people that have fastened their big teeth into every quarter of the globe and flung their big hearts in song at the feet of Nature, and even done both things at the same time. The man who wrote the most magnificent sentence in the English language was a pirate and died on the scaffold."

And to this day the chief political peculiarity of the English remains the same – lack of insularity. These shores, however green, however pleasant, have not satisfied them. They have always directed their gaze and pointed their beloved vessels outward on the water. Not with any deliberate attempt to conquer and possess and rule, but under the impulse of their natures. They did not look for an Empire, they found one by mistake. I once had the honour of talking with Rudyard Kipling, a poet who in some parts of his work showed special interest in Empire-builders. "I will tell you," he said, "how the English came to rule India. A handful of adventurous armed traders arrived on the east coast of India. In that land of warring tribes it was soon found that wherever these men pitched their tents there was safety – you could go to bed without fear and rise in peace. So for safety's sake more and more natives gathered round them. Finally the tiny circle of their influence spread over the whole country, and the English found themselves in possession of a continent." That was Part I of the story. Kipling also outlined Part II. "It would probably have worked all right to this day," he continued, "if a lot of busybodies had not come along and insisted upon bettering and democratizing and elevating the people. The people must be given a vote, they must be educated and all the rest of it – though they did not want any of those things. And now we see the result."

We can accept that summary of English Imperialism. But nobody who knows the English can be surprised at it, nor imagine that it could have been otherwise. Their nature is such that the making of colonies and the exploitation of colonies for any length of time could never be possible. Like most great nations the English combine opposite characteristics. The Spaniard, Garcia Calderon, advanced the suggestion that the two totally unlike aspects of the English spirit find fitting symbolic representation in the figures of Caliban and Ariel just as the spirit of Spain is represented by Don Quixote and Sancho Panza. The merit of such an approach is that it makes us pause before we dismiss either those who say that England is a nation of shopkeepers or those who say that she is a nation of poets. It is certainly a preventive for those who would use the easy and cheap words hypocrisy or cant or humbug in relation to so complicated a person as the plain Englishman. There is ample data to show that he is practical, cold, short-sighted, cautious, hard-headed, grasping, unimaginative: there is not less data to show that he is idealistic, humanitarian, daring, adventurous, extravagant, high-pitched, imaginative. In my experience the English commercial spirit is alarmingly pronounced. But the idealism is almost as strong. This combination makes the Englishman a not thorough, a not fanatical idealist – and such a person, as all the world knows, is ill-equipped for the carry-out of foreign policies.

1 To call them "distressed areas" is a bad way of trying to minimize and localize the tragedy. Brockway's *Hungry England* or George Orwell's brilliantly informative *Road to Wigan Pier* are essential documents for clearing this up.

4

SOME OF THE PEOPLE AND THEIR CHARACTERISTICS

Once I was obliged to stand for half an hour every week on a platform at New Cross Junction. From this place trains carry passengers to extremely respectable suburbs such as Honor Oak Park, Forest Hill and Sydenham, while other trains carry passengers to the London Docks, to Wapping, Rotherhithe, Shadwell. In the centre of a certain platform is one of those erections which are divided into two alcoves for people to sit down and wait in. One alcove faces the trains going to the suburbs, the other trains going to the Docks. In one sit suburban people, in the other dock people.

I shall always remember those alcoves. The difference between the people was so immense. It was such a photograph of England's class-divisions. England is *the* country for classes and for class-consciousness. With almost oriental anxiety everyone is afraid one way or another of "losing caste."

Not only is there a clear-cut division between an upper, a middle, and a lower class, but there are several varieties of upper, of middle, and of lower classes. These varieties are not superficial, they are absolute. So much so in fact that there is no possible communication to be exchanged between them more than can be carried on over a telephone. I am acquainted with a certain locality in which the small population consists of one upper-middle-class family, one middle-class family, one lower-middle-class family, a few lower-class families, the Vicar and family, and one cultured family. Result – no social life at all. No community. No tea-parties. No conversation save on the weather. It is not a question of ill-will between these classes; merely an inability to mix – the divisions being so real.

Thus those in England who are working for a classless society have their work cut out for them; they will have to do a lot of changing of English nature. This hierarchy is believed in by the people, those at the bottom or half-way down see themselves mounting the ladder at least a few steps before they die. According to Marx this is due to economic conditions. But in so far as all other capitalist countries don't go in for all these classes, it seems possible that Marx may have been wrong. Pending further proof from the Left we must acknowledge I think that this dividing-up of the inhabitants into grades is inherent in the English nature.

I hope it will be realized by the reader of the forthcoming remarks that I am simply giving a few personal impressions and not an exhaustive *account* of English classes. My approach is purely prejudicial and not judicial. My objective remarks and observations are coloured by my subjectivity. I confess that I do not see what value objective remarks can ever have unless they are experiences and therefore subjective. Indeed I would state as a fundamental truth, not always acknowledged, that it is precisely from its personal character that even any philosophy derives its objective value. Of course there are and for some purposes ought to be exhaustive accounts of such things – though to make them complete seems rather impossible. Anyway that is obviously not in my line, so I'll proceed with my prejudices – starting with the working man.

I find it difficult to like him, and easy to like the gentleman. I'm afraid that may dish me straight away with any gentle reader I may possibly have. For the English gentleman has a very great regard for the British working man, or thinks he has, and certainly is determined to have. The English gentleman is no snob. He is the only person in England who is not a snob. He feels class-conscious far less than anyone – indeed I have noticed with surprise how often he fails to sense the class-consciousness of others. Not harbouring it himself he does not read it into others even when it is written all over their persons. When it does come up before him he wants to abolish it. It is he who is most often responsible for talk of "the classless society." He detests waiters, hall-porters, tailors, flunkeys of all sorts; he loathes being helped on with his overcoat – it makes him feel embarrassed. The public school and university man can be instantly recognized by the way in which he treats persons of lower station as persons and not as persons of lower station, by his general courtesy, and especially by his easy way of getting on with servants of all kinds, chaffing them, ragging them, joking with them in a spirit of bonhomie totally lacking amongst the lower-middle-classes. He does not like inequalities, and wishes the whole country were composed of ladies and gentlemen. He sees social progress as a process of levelling *up*.

When he has to speak of the "lower classes" he apologetically puts the words in inverted commas to show that it is only a manner of speech. In recent years he has even taken to calling the London charwoman a charlady: a small point but telling, for it would be difficult to conceive of any person less like a lady than the often very delightful Cockney charwoman (the occasional fallen-from-better-days type who mince the lady, are holy terrors). Further, it must be added that many members of the middle class who are most conscientious and most vocal do not even believe in any possible levelling up. They appear to have lost all confidence in themselves and their values. They do not think that they themselves are any good; they feel that it would be grand to be on an equal footing with the proletariat (who every year more and more cease to exist); they satirize each other as "bourgeois" (a very silly modern swear-word); they invert snobbery; they declare that their own education is worthless; they regard a high standard of thought and interest as rotten compared with a labourer playing darts; and they no longer believe in their own best traditions. It is open to question whether such a gutless attitude can have valuable results. To say: "Owing to my bringing-up I am better than the grocer's assistant and am determined to work for a society in which he will be as good as I" is not a happy way of putting it nor a good platform remark, but it does not reek with the canting negativity of saying: "It is ridiculous for my absurd bourgeois self to pretend that I am superior to the grocer's assistant" – an attitude which seems to be becoming common and is accepted by the working man, who loathes any form of culture, hates superior qualities, and looks up only to superior incomes.

Perhaps I may be forgiven my prejudice against the British working man on the simple ground that I come from Ireland. The poor man in Ireland is seldom poor in spirit or address. No matter how "low" you look there you find something aristocratic in him. He can be as mean about money or as money-grabbing as anyone else, but lack of riches does not spell poverty of soul. He commands respect by his natural dignity of mien. At his best he is an obvious nobleman, and even at his worst there is a sort of fallen splendour about him. He responds to quality. He understands quantity no less than others, but possessing quality himself, he salutes it in others. He often has much poetry in his heart and on his tongue. He is intelligent; he will talk to you instantly on general affairs, not only concerning Ireland either – Abyssinia, Spain or whatever – and he will throw in a theory about Lloyd George or Erskine Childers. He is hospitable. He can be loyal, grateful and affectionate. He is splendidly an individual. He is religious. Possessing these qualities and being fairly free from the dreadful farce of modern education, he has made a little culture of his own in Europe. It is easy to like such men (to use no warmer word) and such women. It is easy to look forward to meeting them. It is too easy to hope profoundly that they will come to no harm.

The virtues of the English working man are well known: good nature, decency, cleanliness, self-respect, ironic humour, patience and a capacity to rub along in family life which puts the middle classes to shame. He has far more civil virtues than the Irish and less murder in his heart. But neither has he poetry in his soul. He does not respond to quality. He is unintelligent. He is not interested in the world outside himself. Aristocracy of spirit makes no appeal to him whatever, while he has an unholy reverence for aristocracy of wealth. Men with European reputations are not in the least looked-up to in their neighbourhoods unless they have made a lot of money as well. In Russia, in Ireland, the man who had thought and fought for mankind with his pen is revered by the people. But only money impresses the English working man. In Ireland a gentleman is at once recognized and treated as such by the natural gentlemen and women of the land – in England that quality cannot be seen where the manifestation of money-power is lacking. The "sturdy independence" of this working man is the arrogance of one who having the slave mind, the slave worship, and the slave character yet wishes to believe that "I'm as good as 'e is" – though he does not really believe it, feels that the superiority lies elsewhere, and would gladly desert his own class and become a gentleman. Outside his own family he recognizes no such words as loyalty, gratitude or affection. His emotional reactions to politeness, decency, thoughtfulness, fair dealing and generosity differ radically from those of the gentleman. He will return prolonged kindness with unkindness, and good doing with evil doing. He will turn round on you at any moment. As soon as it suits him he will let you down no matter how often you may have let yourself down on his account. He is irreligious to the core. He loathes the very idea of culture, and if ever he did any dictating he would trample underfoot the little of it there is.

Hence it is extremely difficult to make contact with him as a human being – a fact widely recognized and bewailed by the upper classes. Indeed, if anyone achieves this contact he is considered one up on his fellows and is careful to let them know about it – "Just been to the pub and had a good chat with the locals." It is perhaps not very difficult to achieve that much or even to get to the stage of calling them by their Christian names, "Alf," "Bert" and so on – provided this is done through a game of darts. But to "be accepted by them," to use the phrase of the aspiring democrats from the upper classes, is another matter. If ever there was an out-and-out English gentleman it was Edward Carpenter – who was also an out-and-out democrat from the heart.

"I confess," he said, "that I love a *dirty* hand." And it was a private ambition of his to be called by his Christian name in the local pub. He succeeded in this after thirty years.

The gentleman is inclined to assume that this failure to make contact is his fault. It is a hasty assumption. For one can only make contact with a mind, an intelligence, a soul, a character, an individual alive to interests outside money, gambling, darts, the Royal Family and the personal concern. From the "common man" of other countries the mental worker can come away enriched. But not from this man.[1] Nor is there any question of looking forward to meeting him (unless one is residing amongst the lower-middle class). His lack of interest in politics is remarkable considering how much political agitation goes on concerning him. As aristocracy of wealth is the only kind he recognizes, he is too material-minded to be an equalitarian. He compromises and goes all out for liberty instead of equality. To be free is a much hollower achievement than to be equal; but it is possible of achievement, and engenders self-respect and saves face. And he is given as much of it as possible. "Freedom" is recognized as something to which every Englishman is entitled. If only a man is brave enough on any given occasion to "stand up for his rights," he will receive no injury when it comes to the point – the soldiers will not touch him, and the authorities will admire him. He is content to be free to obey the law. But the law must give him scope to indulge in the most dignified and the most telling of all forms of action – the Strike. Possessing this, he wants to leave all general political ideas aside.

Exceptions to all the above? Of course, but I find it impossible to persuade myself that the exceptions unbalance the generalization. The very warmth with which one regards the exceptions one meets is itself a suspicious circumstance. Though of course I know that now that I have written down the above, I shall go into a pub and find everyone incredibly decent and good-natured; I will go into the street and ask the way from some robust woman selling papers, and she will say: "First on your right, dear," or ask a group of men who will say: "It's only five minutes' walk, mate." And I will wish I had not said what I have said.

Incidentally, as regards that word Mate. It is doubtful whether there will ever come a time in England when the term Comrade or Citizen or Friend will go down well. Colleague even stands a better chance. But the word Mate is held in reserve as a possibility, and is the only one that is occasionally used spontaneously. Unfortunately I have to acknowledge that the only really conspicuous occasion upon which I was called by that title was when it was used as a *rebuke*. I had been fingering some grapefruit at a stall. None of them seemed to me particularly ripe, and I felt them over. This did not please the owner, who regarded me with much irritation. "That's all right, mate," he said, "take one and leave t'others."

2

The measure of the general disappointment felt by the upper classes in being able to make so little contact with the working man is a guarantee of the respect in which he is held. Whether he opens up or not, whether he remains exclusive, it is felt as a relief to be with him after leaving any of the lower-middle-class grades. The workmen are in touch with reality. Though they hanker after cheap respectability they are still real. But the moment another step in the social ladder is mounted you find battalions who live at least one remove from reality all their lives. Hence there is not much competition to socialize with them. This is perhaps where an exhaustive account would come in handy. A treatise drawn up by some hundred-per-cent observer, marking off the divisions of the various grades, would make an interesting study. It would be worth fixing definitely the exact grade to which those belong who during a conversation with an acquaintance or a neighbour or a friend keep calling him *Mr* So-and-So. "Good afternoon, Mr Stewart. Weeding the lawn? That's right. Just a little bit every day, Mr Stewart, and the thing is done. You don't want to break your back. Yes, hasn't it, but then there's no use complaining, is there, Mr Stewart, if it rains it rains and that's all about it. Well, I suppose I must go on now and do my own little bit as I always say. Good afternoon, Mr Stewart." The fact that she (or he) introduces this Mr at intervals during any conversation, divides her off dead from the upper-middle-class and the lower-class, but does it fix her as upper-lower-class or as lower-middle-class or as upper-lower-middle-class or as lower-upper-middle-class or simply as middle-middle-class? A grave question, not to be answered lightly, for this insistence upon the Mr is an insistence upon the fact that the speaker is above a certain grade. It would be also worth getting clear as to the exact geographical position in this hierarchy of the person whom I have frequently heard described in England as "not quite a lady, but *a lady in her mind.*"

Before passing on it is perhaps permissible to add that there is a good deal of individuality in all these classes (especially in the working classes) amongst the men – but little amongst the women. My impression is that the women differ hardly at all – though each grade is different. But not as individuals. I have known as many as five women in a village who looked exactly alike physically and whose every thought, motive and deed could be chalked up beforehand. Wherever you go, up and down these grades, you find women incredibly similar, each overwhelmingly material and clean, and with husbands very much nicer than themselves. Their power over their female children is tremendous, overwhelming. They are like great walls of *will* against which the daughters beat in vain, and become at last exactly like their mothers – hence the lack of individuality amongst these women. But while making these rather unchivalrous reflections I do not forget that the women in England below a certain level are still slave-driven to a shocking extent – there has not been much socialism for them! And there are no Trade Unions for housewives! The working man has no sex problem, no woman problem, no domestic problem on the scale these problems rage elsewhere. This does something to account for his lack of sympathy for and his disloyalty to Edward VIII – the one King who spoke as a democrat. The working men simply didn't understand his difficulty or need, and said with a moral indignation equal to the contemptuous ingratitude which every wise man learns to expect from them – "Can't 'ave any of that there 'ere."

It is necessary to go to the upper and upper-middle classes to find the Englishman who has impressed himself on the world. It is idle to suppose that Strube's "Little Man" could ever have done that. And that little fellow is no idle abstraction; today he makes up a large proportion of the population. He is a miserably mild little man, no empire-builder. He is down-trodden, without spirit or say. He hates to speak above a whisper in strange company. He'll do anything to "avoid a scene." With imploring eyes he will ask a railway porter a question, and be terribly grateful if the man doesn't (though he generally does) take it as a personal insult to be asked anything. He is the easy victim of the restaurant proprietor who charges 2s. 6d. for *eggs* and bacon and puts *one* egg and one piece of bacon before him. He is the prey of the million lodging-house and hotel keepers who tell him "I want to be fair" while determining to be as unfair as possible. He is chased off every kind of grass with the greatest facility. He is the fodder upon which the quacks, the charlatans and the play-actors of the commercial world, of the insurance world, of the legal world, and of the chemist-shop world feed. And when he goes into Woolworth's to buy something for sixpence, he feels no resentment when the girl refuses *even to start wrapping up* the article until he has handed over the money.

To find the Englishman who can make more of an impression than this we must go to the Gentleman. I do not subscribe to the peculiar idea that gentlemen are not found in other countries as well, or were even "invented" in England. Good breeding, as far as my experience goes, has much the same manifestations everywhere. Nevertheless there is something very solid and definite and English about the public school and university man who has made such an impression on the world.

He is generally spoken of as the product of these public schools. They are supposed "to turn out a particular type." The phrase may lack final profundity. For we must remember that the schools themselves are created, are "turned out" by human beings. The characteristics of the English people are responsible for the public schools rather than the other way round: the schools are the effect not the cause. So when we hear someone talking about "the best traditions of our great public schools" we must realize that he means "the best traditions of our national character."

But I must avoid dogmatism on this point. We have clearly two truths here. And they are the kind of truths which everyone who calls himself a Marxian and embraces the materialistic conception of history should be invited to consider. We must remember that, as Oscar Wilde put in, Nature copies Art. Anyway human nature does. Men set up, says Dr Ernest Barker in his book on National Character, Law and Government, Religion, Language and Literature, Education. "Men make these great and august things, and these great and august things in turn make men. We are made by what we have made. We project our ideas into the world of reality, and when they have taken shape and form, they shape and form us by their reaction upon us." And later he adds: "Mr Kipling's pictures of the men who have made the British Empire have helped to make the men who have made the Empire." In the same way Englishmen have made the public schools, and the public schools now make them. Yet not for ever. It seems to me that the amount of laughter in recent years at "the Old School Tie" is beginning to undermine their influence and their creative ability. Not more than a year ago a play was put on in the West End in which the author seriously adopted an extreme public school attitude, and it had to be taken off because the riot of laughter with which it was greeted every night finally got beyond control.

Are the usual remarks made about the public schools true? We must suppose so, to a large extent. But it's funny the way ridiculous remarks are taken as true. "More attention is paid to games than to work," for instance. I was at Rugby, and I cannot say that I noticed that. True, there were a lot of games, and those who played them well enjoyed themselves more than others – in what schools, male or female, is this not the case? (And we must remember that happiness at school depends neither upon work nor games, but is almost entirely a question of whether you have friends or not – which at that age means love and ecstasy.) We had to work morning, noon and night. Games were merely a relief, and a great relief, from this. At least they were a relief to me, because I don't possess "school-brains." Did one learn anything? I don't understand the question. What has anyone ever learnt at school that he has not forgotten immediately? Learning is not possible or necessary at that age. But the mind can be exercised and developed so that when it comes of age it is in a sufficiently athletic state to tackle Knowledge. Moreover, if the mind is well exercised and strengthened and fed on hard material it will be a good servant for imagination, which only begins to develop about the age of twenty to twenty-five. In any case, talent probably thrives better under resistance than under assistance. In this respect the work at Rugby seems to me very sound. In my own case I was kept off luxuriating in literature and history until, years later, I was ready to take them up. I was certainly never "put off ever reading Shakespeare" by the way we "did" him once in a while, and I am convinced that anyone who could be put off Shakespeare or Wordsworth in this way will confer a benefit upon himself and others if he never at any time attempts to read those writers.

The accustomed observation that the public schools are chiefly concerned with the creation of character is true. As Meredith was right in pointing out that boys have no character, this is not difficult. What actually happens is that the boys join a Church, the creed of which they can believe in and appreciate no less than the Chinese could embrace Confucianism. Christ is not held up for imitation, but rather the ideal of the Decent Fellow whose attributes are honesty, good form, stoicism, loyalty, reserve, fair play and so on.

Volumes could be written upon what is implied and carried out in the name of those hackneyed words. It is unnecessary to expand them, they can be taken as known. But if ever these traditions are undermined or really laughed out of court by those wearing the New School Tie of modernism, it will be a bad day for England. For they are magnificent traditions (in spite of some drawbacks), and not less so because they are taken for granted and serve daily as a practical substitute for the official ideal of Christianity. It is a Church of England of a most workable kind.

Take a single example – Honesty. If you deal with a man who is not a gentleman in England you have to take every precaution, to be suspicious, to safeguard yourself against being done in the eye. And you are right in doing so if you are dealing on any sort of commercial footing; for if he is not a gentleman he will, today, nine times out of ten, be a liar, a charlatan, a backbiter and a thief under a respectable covering. If he were an Arab you could count upon his not playing you false in many important ways – for the Koran forbids it, and the Koran is obeyed. The Bible means nothing to the man who isn't a gentleman and little to the man who is. But the latter has his own working bible, his traditions. And he sticks to them. The public schools may not be "fair" places from the privileged point of view, but they have bestowed supreme values upon English life. They have created superior men. The man whose word is taken as a bond more valuable than a piece of paper is a superior being. "Even in walking through rarely visited parts of Central Africa," says H W Nevinson, "I have found it sufficient to tell my carriers that I would give them each so many lengths of calico per week or per month. Simply because I was an Englishman they took my word without hesitation." Such an imponderable as this can hold an Empire together.

The fact that there is often an amusing and satire-inviting side to the principles of this Church, does not mean that they are silly – only that they are fallibly practical rather than impossibly ideal. Once, on horseback, I rode a man down in Richmond Park. As I assisted him to his feet I apologized as best I could. Instead of abusing me, he shook me by the hand almost exactly as if it were the end of a boxing bout. It was in the best tradition of our great public schools. But of course, Stoicism, as interpreted by Englishmen, can be carried too far. To control the primitive self and the passionate self on all occasions and confront the world with as unemotional an exterior as possible, banishing from the face signs of fear, annoyance, dislike or affection; to refuse to take offence or give offence; to carry delicacy of feeling so far that few topics of conversation can safely be broached at all in view of possible intellectual or moral embarrassment; to be as reserved as possible about everything lest it might be thought that you have "betrayed a confidence" or lest something said "might be interpreted as the betrayal of a confidence"; never to hurt anyone's feelings or self-respect, and if you do anything against someone say that "there's nothing personal in it," and if you want to kick a man out of some institution "invite him to resign"; never say what you mean or what you really think if it is unflattering: these and other principles of a similar kind all make towards the attainment of an exceedingly high degree of civilization. The worst of it is that they tend to produce humanitarianism rather than humanity. To be inhumanly humanitarian is regarded as a fault outside England. To say or do the wrong thing spontaneously on occasion is not considered elsewhere as being always inferior to saying and doing the correct thing on principle. Hence the question as to whether the English gentleman is quite human is continually under discussion, sometimes even whole books being devoted to this one question.

Yet I often think that these particular principles are themselves a spontaneous *need* for the English gentleman who strikes me as being extraordinarily shy and sensitive. You pay a visit to some well-known great man, perhaps a man of European reputation in Letters, and you find that even here the preliminary shy conversation has to be gone through almost as if it were a ritual; you must say whether or not you found it easy to discover the house and the street, after which there follows a short discussion concerning the distance and merits of the local railway service and other long irrelevancies, while you say to yourself – Even this man seems to be tied up inside! Why the English gentleman should so shrink into himself and make unwritten laws to facilitate his so doing is not clear. Underneath he is like other human beings: remember that earthquake which went on for years in the shape of D H Lawrence, whose *cri de cœur* was for spontaneity and who got such a tremendous response for carrying sexual discussion to the extreme possible limit in *Lady Chatterley's Lover*; witness the intense suggestiveness of the magazines – in spite of the fact that the authorities burnt 40,000 foreign ones the other day as being too inflammatory for the English; and recall the reception accorded to the incredibly unEnglish broadcast by the exiled King.

Of course the stiff, unemotional type may have been more typical of the Victorian Age than of any other. It is amazing how representative a representative man like Gladstone appears for his age, as Baldwin does for this age. One feels that only a Victorian Englishman could have been so foolish with the Queen. Completely to forget the fact that she was a woman, and that the point about women is that they are more human than men, would seem only possible to a Victorian Englishman like Gladstone, who introduced no feeling into his reports to the Queen simply because it was not a written-down requirement. The result is that this fine man is made to appear in the eyes of posterity at a disadvantage beside that consistently self-interested woman.

Why the pressing back of warm feelings and the rejection of risky subjects like sex became an ideal is not certain. But there is no getting away from it that such an ideal is one of the characteristics of the English gentleman. I once witnessed a striking example of this. During the War I spent a time in the Inns of Court Training Battalion before joining the Irish Guards. In my tent, into which about twelve of us were crowded, there was one public school man from Rugby. I found that the conversation of everyone except him was concerned with one subject only – sex. I was surprised to learn that it was the only subject in the world. But the public school boy never once joined in this bawdy talk. I responded to him. For I also recoil from the smutty joke. On the other hand I recognize that those who tell smutty stories are often far healthier sexually than those who shrink from them. The tent was full of healthy barbarians. My friend was not a barbarian but he went to the other extreme which could not possibly be described as healthy. Later on

I shared some "digs" with him at Berkhampstead, and those who visited us there always kissed the landlady's daughter. It wasn't till the last hour of the last day that my friend saw that he ought to do this – and then he missed his direction and kissed her ear by mistake. And though he was eighteen it was only by listening attentively to the conversation of his companions that he learnt for the first time how the sexual act was performed.

There is no exaggeration about this case. It was the direct result of his public school's attitude to sex – I know this, as I was his contemporary. At that time Dr David was Headmaster, a tremendously moral man. One summer term he undertook a "purge" on an almost dictator-like scale. He expelled nearly a hundred boys for sexual malpractice. Dr David was not good in the pulpit, but on the platform in front of boys he was more impressive than anyone I have ever heard. He made us feel corrupt and vile. To my dying day I shall remember how, standing before the stricken audience of the whole school, he said: "If you have done it, if you do it, bear it *in silence and in shame.*" The boys who did it less furtively were expelled. I have often wondered what happened to them. For at that age such a disgrace is like a knife in the soul, and many parents must have behaved abominably to their "ruined" sons. The headmaster was made a bishop.

But this was twenty years ago. Times change. The writer on England today cannot pretend that these things are still the same. I believe that twenty years of the new psychology has altered the English educated man. The Puritan ideal has been killed. In many quarters there is a cynical unshockability which goes to the other extreme. And we must remember that the repressed Englishman has provided the Freudians with their happiest hunting-ground. The result is great self-consciousness in this matter. Perhaps his famous "reserve" is also breaking down. I hope not. Gabblers can be found at any time and in any place – the man with the gift of silence is rare. And I may add that I have personally never found an Englishman unwilling to talk on profound or intimate subjects provided one approached the matter with the tact of a doctor announcing the death of a near relation.

However, apart from the traditions which are changing and the traditions which have an awkward or a funny side, they are the finest conceivable substitute for a believed-in religious creed of conduct. And now that those other standards have gone from the religious foundation, these traditions attain more value than ever. When great intelligence happens to be added to these qualities, we find the really superior man whose inborn idealism never becomes cant and whose inborn decency never becomes puritanism. It is my privilege to know such men and to know that they are unbeatable. I do not believe that humanity yet reaches higher than the intelligent English gentleman. I need not add that there is no one higher than he in England. I have heard people say: "I am a middle-class man" – which proves that he doesn't quite succeed in being a gentleman (no one has ever been heard to say that he is a lower-middle-class man). A gentleman does not say that he belongs to the upper classes, because he does not know what the words really mean – but he does not and cannot acknowledge any superiority in the titled person.

Even when the above qualities and principles inform the otherwise hollow man they are impressive. A man whose actual mind on its own is as much a blank as a room TO LET, but who has it furnished for him with these traditions, is a capital fellow. "For God's sake leave it in the hands of a gentleman anyway," people say, knowing that though he will probably be stupid he will not be low. Hence the English army man is as nice a person as you can meet anywhere. Hence Rowing or Rugger Blues often get invitations from bishops asking them to join the Church of England. The bishops realize that the English do not want intellectuality or spirituality in their Church, for they are not a religious people, they are an ethical people. Hence it is better that their clergymen should consist of morally elevated athletes than men with religious experience.

3

It seems to me, therefore, that as people cannot be levelled up beyond a certain point, English reformers should hesitate before deciding to get rid of the gentleman and level everyone down – for though in the eye of justice the gentleman occupies an unfair position, he is responsible for the superiority of the English people in the world. Nor is that all. From the point of view of making practical headway, of getting things done, of arriving at results without undue friction, the public school tradition acts as a supreme value in four ways: in making Parliament workable, in running a Civil Service, in keeping down militarism with its concomitants, and in making socialistic progress.

In these days the parliamentary system proves itself impossible if passions, hatreds and offensive remarks are allowed. The system is cracking up on the Continent. In England it still goes strong on account of the personal superiority of the gentlemen in the House. It does not break down because, however critical the times, the spirit of the House is one of fair play, give and take, inoffensiveness, courtesy, gentlemanliness between all parties. The House, as I said before, considers itself a unity – however highly tensioned it may be. The Opposition opposes the measure brought forward from the other side of the House, and the matter is thoroughly thrashed out. The captain of this opposing side (often called Leader) has just been offered a thousand pounds a year extra by his opponents as a token to his sportsmanship.

It is therefore not surprising to learn that the rough diamonds who go to Westminster deciding "to change all this" and bring about sweeping revolutionary measures are warned by experienced hands against "the air of the House of Commons." That warning is needed, but it is in vain. For as soon as the Labour Members breathe this atmosphere it seems to them natural and admirable – the spirit of the aristocrat is stronger than the spirit of the plebeian, and the greater overcomes the less. A subtle change begins to work in the latter, until he too adopts the same outlook as those whom he has been warned against. David Kirkwood, a fearless Left-winger in the House, and valiant fighter for the rights of the class he knows best, the working class, tells how he soon found that the atmosphere of sincerity, non-hatred, goodwill, simplicity and unaffectedness which he met with in the biggest men, won him over from regarding them as mortal enemies to be abused. Indeed to abuse Ministers was useless. T P O'Connor, an Irishman who became gradually more English than the English and was therefore rewarded by being called "the Father of the House," said to Kirkwood after the latter had made a crude attack: "Don't do that sort of thing! I've been through it. It does no good. You might as well stick pins in a crocodile. They will listen to argument, but abuse does not interest them." He found this to be true. He could *not* get his opponents to take offence, to show resentment, or to be hurt by what he said. He attacks Neville Chamberlain. The latter does not reply or hit back in any way. Five days later he comes up to Kirkwood in the Lobby and asks him what he, Chamberlain, had said to hurt him. "I had meant to hurt him," declares this honest Scot, "and he was only concerned about how *he* had hurt me!" That is the public school spirit. Kirkwood shouts at Baldwin bitterly: "Man, vain man, drest in a little brief authority. You think you are a giant. You are nothing but a Uriah Heep!" Again, Baldwin, instead of hitting back, buttonholes him in the Lobby afterwards and asks: "Do you really think I am a Uriah Heep? Have I appeared like that to you?" And again Kirkwood is floored by this big way of taking an insult. That is the public school spirit. It might be called by the loftier name of – wisdom. For the man of action, the man who wants to see results, is wise who refuses to let irrelevant insults or personalities retard progress. But there is no element of guile about it. This wisdom is instinctive and therefore innocent.

Mark that place called the Lobby, by the way. When Members are in this place they feel that they have more in common as Englishmen than as party men. In their old age they love to tell anecdotes of what was said here following some stormy scene on the floor of the House, beginning with: "Afterwards I met him in the Lobby, and do you know what he said?..." Also it is regarded as a good place to retire to sometimes to save embarrassment. This was much in evidence during the recent debate on the delicate question of raising the salaries of the teams. Everything went smoothly enough, but it was natural that in the course of the evening a few indelicacies of statement should be made by Northern Members. One of them was so unparliamentary in phraseology as to say that the scramble for Cabinet position owing to the monetary reward was a sorry sight and that "it produced the lowest type." Those concerned personally with this insult, seeing what was coming, managed to be in the Lobby at the moment, while any who remained on the benches engaged themselves in conversation of some obviously amiable and humorous kind with no bearing on the subject in hand. For silence, be it noted, is not enjoined on Members in the House as it is in their clubs. Thus a hum of conversation often goes on throughout the entire speech of some unfortunate Honourable Member who cannot hold attention, or who, as in the above case, was saying unEnglish things. This is recognized as a traditional way of dealing with speakers to whom retorting would be undignified. Some Members even regard it as part of their duty "to keep up a buzz of conversation just loud enough to prevent a given speaker from being intelligible." I cannot conceive a harder place to make a successful speech in than the House of Commons.

The public school tradition is responsible for the renowned excellence of the Civil Service. Its conscientious, brilliant, self-effacing teamwork is the envy of the world. Here the ideal of devotion to duty and of "unheroically doing your job" as part of a team is brought to perfection. It requires brilliant abilities to get into the Civil Service; but these men receive no applause from the multitude, they take no part in the personality stunt of Westminster — yet they do not mind, they know that the country could not get on without them. It is here, I think that one finds the purest expression of the particularly English genius — unsurpassed capacity for *administration*. At the fresh enterprise, the subtle organization, and the political arrangement they are easily surpassed by the Scots from whom England draws tremendous strength.

I often wonder how the English would have got on without their friendly Northern neighbours. The gifted Scot has an uncanny power of being in direct, visual, concrete touch with the imponderable considerations in Business and Intrigue which are in the end the vital factors. The genius of the Scottish people does not lie in the realm of self-sacrifice and idealism. It lies in the realm of realism. For all other people in the world there intervenes a film between the subject and the object. For the Scot there is no film. Between him and reality nothing intervenes. He is in direct contact with his object. He is indeed uncanny. Listen to an Englishman and a Scot debating: the former will be convinced of his own rightness or blasély on the defensive, while the latter will be *in contact with* the matter in hand. It makes an immense impression. The result is that the moment we hear that a Scot is doing such and such a piece of work, we know it is all right. His plane is not the spiritual, nor the sensual, nor the ideal. It is the material. There he is supreme. There also he is innocent because he is natural – while a similar emphasis taken up by others would give an impression of positive Satanism.

In making full use of the Scottish power of subtle organization and political astute understanding of how to sit on the fence, and in not refusing to take full advantage of the Welsh gift for making wonderful material advance under cover of pseudo-piety, the English show their wisdom again. For they know how to remain masters in their own house. They know that though they do most of the humbler work themselves, they are not the hirelings.

I come to the third advantage of the public school spirit. It is the best bulwark England has against the unholy trinity of Militarism, Fascism and Anti-Semitic Bullying. Militarism is regarded by some strong modern nations as a good. In so far as order is good militarism is good. But order cannot be considered as an absolute. Man has the right to consider disorder as preferable to the lowest kind of order – which is militarism. As a principle it is the negation of personality and is therefore a step backwards in evolution. And even though it may produce order, it gives opportunity for the expression of primitive passions which we are trying to leave behind. Cruel men, knowing that they will not be held responsible for what they do, can be cruel in the name of authority. Systems of iron and methods of blood can always be justified in the name of military necessity. The moment we subordinate ourselves to this we know that we have stepped outside civilization and can no longer claim property in even our own souls. "Surely at no period in the world's history," wrote an English leader of thought of immense learning, twenty-three years ago, "has it been so necessary as it is today to strike hard at militarism. Never before has it been so clearly visible that all civilization, even all the most elementary traditions of humanity and brotherhood, depend on the absolute destruction of militarism." I do not say that in Germany and Italy now there is not a certain fine sense of brotherhood amongst the young fascists and nazis; but what mercy have they upon all those who shrink from militarism? The kindly, sentimental Germans, today as yesterday, are made to bear the yoke of Prussian taskmasters.

This suppression of individuality and the making of the *thing* more important than the *person* is against the spirit and the traditions of the English gentleman. There are heaps of touts and roughs in England who would like to give rein to their cruelty and violence and to the ghastly passion for exercising *unfair* advantage over single individuals. But the public school men would not support them.[2] That's a sure thing! Rather than tolerate it they would wipe out those roughs. From the view-point of Justice – in the reign of which no civilization has yet existed, and which in life nowhere reigns – the public schools are unfair privileges enjoyed by the rich. That is true. Nevertheless they make a very valuable contribution to the whole nation, and they may yet live to save many people from other sorts of injustice and wrong.

Finally I would say that qualities of the English gentleman all go to make him a man with an extraordinarily tender social conscience. He does not forget that he enjoys advantages not shared by the working man. When he writes about the working man he insists always that the latter is the salt of the earth (I think he is a little bit confused and alarmed by *quantity* in this matter: he feels somehow that the large numerical number of working men makes them more virtuous.) He is far more often the brilliant pioneer of social reform than the workers themselves, while his generosity of thought towards them is never reciprocated. The best example of the English gentleman's attitude is provided by Mr H W Nevinson, who regards it even "as an impertinence" on his part to write about the hardships of the working man since his own life compared with theirs has been so easy and pleasant. He says "it seems mean and unworthy to criticize the innumerable classes that have enjoyed no advantages such as mine have been" – though even he cannot stand or understand their disloyalty to the "obligations of promise and engagement." His attitude is a pretty general one. Social conscience is so tender in England that extremists find it a nuisance – the rich are too ready to pay heavy ransom for their privileges.

4

Therefore those who would like to see England continue to carry on in her own famous way, neither Red nor White, but with red, white and blue in her veins as on her flag, should accept the public school type as a valuable means to that end.

Not that I much like using here the word *type*. And before winding up my reflections on the English gentleman by touching on his attitude to sport (I mustn't forget to work in a word on Sport!) I would like to point out that the gentleman is much less of a type than anyone else in the country. In dress, in manner, in action, in thought he often glories in an individuality and an unconventionality that would scare the members of the other classes, all of whom are afraid of doing or thinking anything that might not be considered quite respectable. George Santayana is wrong in showing surprise when he asks "Where else would a man inform you with a sort of proud challenge that he lived on nuts, or was in correspondence through a medium with Sir Joshua Reynolds, or had been disgustingly housed when last in prison?"

It is certainly not as a type that the intelligent gentleman sees himself, but as a highly individual person unlike anyone else. Hence the man who was born almost dead, remaining half-blind and scrofulous, and difficult to rear in spite of his great muscular strength; the man who from the age of twenty had fits of mental ill-health, an inherited melancholy bringing on dejection, gloom, despair, sense of guilt and fear of death; the man who physically had "seldom a single day of ease"; the man who had a fundamental nervous abnormality; the man whose body swayed to and fro as he sat in his chair; the man who flung out his arms in all directions to the alarm of those passing in the public way; the man whose feet performed complicated gyrations; the man who was compelled to touch every lamp-post as he walked down Fleet Street; the man whose feelings were crude and ungoverned and explosive; the man whose linen was dirty and whose manners were coarse; the man who was disgusting when he ate, and who drank a hundred cups of tea a day; the man whose brilliant common-sense wise-cracks were often spoilt owing to the offence he gave by rudeness – this man, an Eccentric of eccentrics, is still continually spoken of as a great representative Englishman.

England is justly famous for being an asylum not only for exiles but also for cranks. The latter receive their chief support from the gentry. Hence nudism (not that there is anything cranky about it save the –ism idiocy) goes to a popular extreme. But I should be unfaithful to my experience if I did not add that the manner in which Morality presides over this movement is impressively English. The propaganda for it insists that the removing of clothes does not stimulate sexual desire. This melancholy slogan, this peculiar and deadly thing to insist on even if it were true, as it is in herds; this outrageous ideal simply proves that the funeral of Mr and Mrs Grundy must be considered as indefinitely postponed. Here they are again – unclothed and in their wrong minds.

5

The qualities which we have been attributing to the English gentleman though pleasant are not very warm and bright ones. But they are marvellously well suited to his main desire – that of being active and never passive. An Englishman wants to act, not to think. That is why there is such an unexampled interest taken in Hamlet's case, the man who remained *inactive*, the man who wouldn't get a move on and murder his relations. That is why Asquith came in for such stinging unpopularity simply because he wanted to *wait and see* before acting hastily. That is why even when a measure is brought forward for debate in the House of Commons it is called a *motion*. I speak under correction and with limited experience, but I think I am right in claiming that the British are the most business-like people in the world. They are wonderful at committee meetings and board meetings for dispatching the matter in hand. Once I had occasion to sit round a table with an American chairman called Mr Legate, to discuss certain programmes. I would put a question to him, and he would always make the same reply in that slow American drawl which goes so incongruously with the nation's ideal of making it snappy: "Before I answer that question, Mr Collis, I would like to put before you *three* prop-po-sitions." Such a thing would be unthinkable in England. Here the object is to "get down to business" without delay. That very word Business is derived from the motional word Busyness (though I don't think that the latter is necessarily derived from the word Buzz-buzz).

So long as he is doing something (even if it is only going round in a circle) the Englishman is happy. To see his enjoyment at co-operating in some concern is a pleasure in itself. But I think he completely fails as a human being in his clubs when the day's work is over. The famous London clubs for rich men are undoubtedly terrible places. I have to confess that they finish me off. But, what's more important, I believe that they frighten young Englishmen just as much as they do me: looking round, the young men say to themselves: "I wonder will I ever get like that!" The result is that many of them hastily marry the wrong woman for no better reason than that they have had a vision of themselves in old age as "club bores."

Some of the People and their Characteristics

I fancy that there is no one in the whole world quite so miserable as an Englishman out of a job. Whether he is poor or rich he simply cannot rely upon internal resources for the production of happiness. This is no doubt the reason why he is responsible for the invention of the games which have bestowed so much benefit upon all nations.

It is not wrong to say that the English are *the* sporting nation of the world. But I sometimes wonder whether the full significance of this is acknowledged. They are the one people who consistently regard play in the right spirit. They refuse to regard it as work; they refuse to regard it as a discipline; they refuse to regard it as a question of national prestige; they refuse to take it *seriously*: games have no real significance outside the field of play. Here the English demonstrate their good sense and bear witness to their imperial dignity. On the Continent sport is placed in the same category as militarism. It is a discipline. The winning of an international match is of political importance. In England there is a great deal of excitement when an international match is won or lost, but if it is lost no one really cares, and from a national point of view it has no significance for anyone. The placards in the street about "England's Disaster" are a recognized form of amusement and have never given anyone the slightest political qualm – for the English realize with commendable common sense that the Battle of Waterloo was won on the battlefield of Waterloo. But I have seen the representatives of more than one Continental country weep over the loss of a match as if indeed it was a national disaster and disgrace. Hence it was right for England to come out low in the recent Olympic Games, since she could not possibly take the training for it with the hot-house forced, professional, concentrated, military seriousness accorded to it by the other competitors.

The English often have a way of doing things on a profound plane of Meaning, without realizing it; and nowhere is this more evident than in their conception of sport. In our more lucid moments it is obvious that life is not for *work*, and that our lives are most truly vital at those times when we see life – as the highest Eastern philosophy sees it – as Lila, *play*. When we are physically fit – no bad ideal since we are so physical – and are feeling the free motion of our limbs during some form of sport, we reach an ecstasy of Aliveness which we recognize at once to be as supreme an end as Awareness. It is one of the Supremes. It is as high above commerce and work as Art. Englishmen grasp this so completely, so instinctively that they will never debase it into a serious discipline or a mere national asset. Hence, so long as it is true play they do not mind whether sometimes it is absurd – as on the occasion of their great annual Boat Race when only *two* boats compete!

It is instructive to note what happens to British games when they are taken over by countries which lack the sporting instinct. The English do not believe in play alone, but in *fair* play. A game like Rugby Football can be remarkably twisted from its original purity of intention by a nation such as America in which the idea of fairness is not regarded as a value. "Thou shalt not kick a man when he is down" is the Eleventh Commandment, the addition which it has been the privilege of the English to give to the Ten drawn up by Moses. Rugby Football concentrates on this. For in the game one of the main things is to fall on the ball in spite of the fact that eight or nine men with heavy boots are charging down upon it. Unhesitatingly the opposing player nearest the ball throws himself upon it, knowing that though he may sustain some damage, he will not be deliberately injured. It is magnificent – for the fair-players remember that it is not war, it is sport. Further we may note in this remarkable game that the players are safeguarded against dangerous exhaustion by means of stopping the game every minute. Either the ball is kicked out of the field to the spectators or else the referee on one pretext or another blows a whistle and the play stops for a second or two while eight of each team lean up against each other and the remainder look on. Thus what would otherwise be an impossible contest is humanized and made into a triumph of sport.

To see how true this is we have only to observe how the game has been twisted out of recognition by the Americans who do not know the meaning of sport – or, rather, they dislike it, and just as they have introduced into the world all-in wrestling to make up for the mildness of ordinary wrestling and boxing, so they have turned football into a field of battle so dangerous that the combatants have to come onto the field clad in various pieces of armour. The Americans are unable to perceive that to come out armed automatically reduces the thing from the lofty realm of play to the low realm of fighting – reduces it to absurdity, for if you come out armed at all you might just as well be armed with a gun. And just as Rugby Football symbolizes perfectly the English sporting spirit, so American Football perfectly symbolizes the temper of the United States. In America you do kick a man when he is down. There is a great spirit of goodwill, comradeship and hospitality exchanged between those who are well off; but those who are not well off, those who do not survive the rough life of that machine-cushioned civilization, those who are down, receive no compassion, no chivalry from those above. How can the Americans help it? Their machines have maddened their primitiveness. They are like tigers in a drawing-room. Under the smooth running of their machine-life they boil and ferment. They have had to invent a law like Prohibition in order to smash it in pieces! Hence their multitude of gangsters and bandits, violent public murderers, enemies, robbers, kidnappers, perjurers, double-crossers and baby-killers. Their iron-handed, barbarous press-gang, men of the knife and the jungle, termites of the pen, have announced the end of chivalry and gentlemanliness and sportsmanship. They are infinitely more powerful than the civilized journalists who in vain try to restrain them.

There is no subject more hackneyed than this about the English and fair play, and on that account I'd avoid it if I could. But it is central. It is a national absolute. It radiates out altogether beyond the field of games. "You're a sportsman" someone will say to another when something decent has been done or when an unfair advantage has not been taken. It informs the morality of private and political life. To say that a thing is unEnglish means that it is unsporting. It is not football. It is not cricket.

For cricket, as much as football, provides the prototype of the English attitude – and again the fact that America prefers baseball is of basic significance. Hence it was a really serious business when quite recently some bounders committed the awful solecism of making cricket itself not cricket. The historian must record seriously, even with solemnity, that the bitter feelings aroused by the introduction of body-line bowling nearly wrecked Imperial relationships. Body-line bowling was an attempt to intimidate the batsman by bowling *at him* instead of at the three sticks which he guards. This was objected to not because the Englishman lacks courage (far from it) but because it was not clean fun. Result: an unheard-of rumpus. Everything else was forgotten in the extreme anxiety lest this meant that the sporting spirit of the nation was in disruption.

It is not therefore surprising that in England play is conceived as something on a higher plane than other activities, and that it must on no account be regarded as work. This leads to awkward consequences which are boldly faced up to. The problem of Amateurs versus Professionals cannot be argued about, for logic is ruled out. It is a question of feeling. It is simply felt that sport stands on an even higher plane than commerce. If a man is *indirectly* paid to play a certain game, it is all right – for that is admitting that he ought not to be paid. But if he demands cash down and gives lessons – then he is no gentleman. If he does this he is not asked to leave the country or even give up the game; he is just given a definite status, he becomes a "pro," a man belonging to an inferior class, and debarred from committee meetings and the gentleman's rooms. Hence there are no adult gentlemen boxers, jockeys or association football players.

To protest that to treat unmoneyed men with a genius for a game in this manner is itself unsporting, unEnglish, and not cricket, may be to utter *le mot juste*. But such *thinking* is unEnglish. Here we must be careful to dwell continually in the realm of pure feeling – which is not the realm of Justice. It is felt that sport should be its own reward. Thousands of pounds are taken at the gates of Twickenham for the big matches. The players could get film-star fees, but they only take their expenses. It is preferred to demonstrate that direct power and glory are so precious to men that money power can be waived. To foster this idea is thought to be of greater service than giving everyone a fair chance. Sport must not be taken so seriously that it ceases to be a game and becomes work.

6

Thus when describing English ways and attitudes it is our privilege to rise above logic, to skip sensible connection, and to reside in the region of eccentricity. Which reminds me that in England the word "sport" is also reserved for another activity which is totally lacking in any element of fairness. Hunting can be defended in spite of the fact that a crowd of helping dogs pursuing one selected animal can never be an edifying spectacle. It can be supported on the ground that the hunt itself is such a fine thing, an intrinsic value. Here in property-parcelled England, when the horses approach, farmers throw open their gates, owners of large houses contemplate with no show of disfavour the invasion of their gardens, while even the secretaries of golf clubs preserve their equanimity when the riders are seen skirting a green. This door through which communism enters is so fantastic as to be worth the death of a fox. The difficulty is to find any redeeming feature in pheasant-shooting: indeed it is never without amazement that I come upon a man – generally squat and ugly with a suitable woman by his side – pointing his gun at the copse while a number of hirelings beat the birds out of the undergrowth so that the gunmen may pot at them. (Amusing is the correct word to describe what would happen if one got behind a tree and snipped off one of the snipers.)

That the name of "sport" should be given to this way of passing the time is all the more curious because the English show little hatred for animals. Indeed they are extremely fond of four of them: the dog, the cat, the horse and the donkey. These four claim the whole nation's obedience, loyalty and devotion. Though they have no actual vote they are represented in Parliament, and laws are passed in their favour. The dog is not considered "sacred" like the Indian cow, but as slightly more than human and as superior to inferior persons, to children, to the infirm and to the poor. In a country churchyard I once came upon the following epitaph on a tombstone:

"Here lies One who throughout his short life commanded the Affection of all who were privileged to know Him. Loving, kind, loyal, above all Meanness and Every Evil thought, He lived unceasingly for the welfare of his Household and the glory of his God." It was to a dog. And in England there is no more popular book than Swift's *Gulliver's Travels*, because the horse is therein glorified at the expense of – foreigners. Though the cat is regarded as rather too aloof and intellectual ("My cat never laughs nor cries," wrote Unamuno the Spanish philosopher, "he is always thinking"), it is considered unEnglish to turn him out of a comfortable chair which you wish to sit in. The donkey also undoubtedly makes a very powerful impression. I note that a perspicacious countrywoman of mine has written a public letter[3] showing her surprise that the authorities running the Spanish War propaganda have thought it sufficient in this country to display pictures of stricken women and children, mangled corpses and wrecked homes. She was present at a meeting in the Hampstead Town Hall where a film was shown on Madrid. Seated beside her was a pleasant, good-natured woman. "She showed in no way that her heart had been touched when she saw the pictures of little children lying dead in their coffins. Then when a donkey appeared on the screen picking its way through a shell-holed street, she exclaimed: 'The poor little donkey!' and tears rolled down her cheeks. The donkey in question was being quite kindly treated, but the thought that he was being subjected to the same privations and dangers as the women and children of Madrid stirred her soul to its depths." Obviously if the propagandists just showed dogs, cats, horses and donkeys in the Spanish War the funds would be enormous.

I might add, of course, that there is a certain penetrating justice in that attitude towards the donkey. The Spanish people are responsible for the Spanish War, and not the Spanish donkey. The latter knows not the Left nor the Right. Unlike the ass in the Bible he is dumb and must suffer in silence for the sins of human beings. Nevertheless we know that in England our minds are not entitled to repose in the territory of justice. For the dumbness of the stag, the fox, the hare, the pheasant and the grouse receives no such consideration.

How explain this? That's just what I can't do. I don't understand people – least of all the English. If only I were a psychologist I could hand out the simple word Compensation and all would be well. That explains all contradictions, I have been given to understand. I am glad of that – for less wise people than psychologists often fall into the error of thinking that the word Compensation merely re-states the contradiction.

Before closing I should not omit to recognize that the hare came in for a little protection recently when his electric counterpart was introduced at dog-racing. But I must add that this caused great pain to many people on account of the dogs. "I am not, I hope, a faddist in any shape or form," wrote a lady to one of the daily papers, "nor do I hold opinions about anything. A few sterling principles, that's all. But I do feel strongly about the gross *deception* that is practised night after night on the poor dogs, who have no way of telling that they have been *deceived*."

---

1 A generalization is a generalization of course, and this one does not hold good of the Lancashire man, who is in a category by himself for a vitality and a gorgeous conceit which are infectious.
2 Perhaps I shall be told that this is too optimistic and that the public schools are now the very breeding-ground of young fascists. If this is so then the gentleman – as I understand the term – is no longer being created in England, and the young men of today between the ages of twenty and thirty have altered in kind from those of the preceding generation. (This is not inconceivable.)
3 Margaret O'Flaherty in *The New Statesman*.

5

ENGLAND AND CULTURE

Having enjoyed rehearsing the qualities of the most civilized people in the world, I hope that this chapter, which must be devoted to a sincere effort to give a personally experienced impression of the cultural aspect of the nation, will not turn out unpleasantly on my hands. For it is possible to be civilized without being cultured. That's the great difficulty about England. The wheels of life are beautifully oiled; but there is a fly in the ointment – distaste for Culture.

This applied even to many of those who are cultured. But first let us consider the general attitude of the people. When that courageous airman, James Mollison, decided to fly to the Cape he looked round for a co-pilot, eventually selecting a Frenchman. He naturally received a great many applications for this honour. The following arrived from the Midlands:

> "Dere Sir, – Can you please take me with u on yore flite I am out of work and motor mending and repairing has been my trade and this would be a big chance for me. Here with my letter is an envelope so you can tell me i may come and oblige yours respectfully."

That letter is worth quoting because, so far from it being freakish, it might have been written by almost any garage-hand or small tradesman in England. From the totally self-absorbed lack of imagination with regard to what he was applying for, to the contemptuous disregard whether he used capitals or not; from the spelling and punctuation to the shattering "and oblige" the whole thing is typical. That's how the baker or carpenter writes a note. It is most interesting. For such an epistle expresses an attitude to life no less than more ambitious works such as *Hamlet* or *Faust*. It is obvious that in the opinion of the writer the idea of writing at least correctly is not worth considering, and further, that he counts upon it being an equally absurd value in the eyes of the receiver – in this case Mollison.

We may doubt whether such an attitude towards education is adopted anywhere else in the world. It is new even in England. It is caused by the spread of education. It is the result of passing from illiteracy to literacy. Today the average man knows just enough to make him despise those who know more. It would be difficult to think of a more idiotic system of education than the present practice of forcing everyone to school for eight years and then suddenly snapping the process off at the age of fourteen! It breeds cultural barbarity. It breeds the new man, the mass man, the machine-made man. As England now begins to enter the era of democracy it is he who inherits the earth. True, he is not as rich as the privileged few, but he has one advantage over all except the exceedingly well-to-do – he is weighty in numbers. He is everywhere. Though he cannot pay much he can give enormous accumulated profits to those who serve him. Therefore he is served first: first in the cinema, first in the press, first in the theatre, first in the bookshop, first in the church, first by the architect – and he is allowed to leave the schoolroom at the age of fourteen! No wonder he is carefree in the destruction of beauty, skilful in the ruin of all values above him, ready and willing to commit to the flames any precious thing which it has taken the labour of centuries to unfold. He possesses extra faculties of his own. He has an immediate knowledge of the technical. He can mend and run machines without previous apprenticeship. He is able to follow what is happening in gangster, spy, mystery and detective films which are often incomprehensible to intellectuals. His arrogant contempt for culture is absolutely spontaneous. He understands the workings of his wireless, but if he switches it on by mistake to hear W B Yeats, he cries: "That man gets down my neck!" And he is proud of the reaction. That's the point, he is proud of it. He rejoices in his barbarity and sees himself as the salt of the earth.

In the illiterate days the people respected culture. Now they spit on it. A charwoman in the days of the Brontës would be thrilled at the idea of the girls writing books. Today she is glad and proud to put back the dusted books on the shelf *upside-down*.

2

This growing contempt for culture is not confined to the lower classes. In the last century the middle classes, though they were called philistines by Matthew Arnold, were children of learning and light compared with what they are now. They had a respect for the things of the mind, they even supported the philosopher. Certainly they were never proud of regarding themselves as incapable of philosophy. That is no longer so. On all sides now we hear the comfortable wife and husband declare with ill-concealed complacency – "I am not interested in philosophy, I'm afraid." So all-pervading is this atmosphere that now no one from above even dares to denounce these people, to tell them what they are made of, to show contempt for them. Today no literary or philosophic champion dreams of saying what he thinks, what he knows to be true about the philistines. It must be nearly forty years ago since that great Scotsman, John Davidson, cried: "What shall we say of people who devote their time to reading novels written by miserable, ignorant scribblers – many of them young, uneducated and inexperienced – and who have hardly read a line of Homer or Sophocles or Dante or Shakespeare or Goethe, or even of Wordsworth or Tennyson, who would laugh at the notion of reading and studying Plato or Aristotle or Thomas Aquinas or Bruno or Rossini? Are they not worse than the merest idiots, feeding prodigally upon swinish garbage, when they might be in their father's house enjoying their portion of humanity's spiritual birthright? I know of few things more utterly sickening and contemptible than the self-satisfied smile of Philistine superiority with which many persons tell me, I am not a philosopher. It simply means this, I am a stupid, low, grovelling fool, and I am proud of it."

Recently, during a foreign exchange series of broadcasts, a representative English housewife talked with a representative housewife from Scandinavia. The former while outlining her activities and views, said: "Books are another interest," and added, "but I always knit while reading, so that I may be sure that I am not wasting my time."

3

The intelligentsia make no protest now (they know who has the money). As strong as any of the above impressions made upon me by England as a cultured country is the impression of the way in which the cultured few let themselves down. It is the England intelligentsia who are to blame for their own appalling plight today.

The general levelling down of intelligence which we have been speaking of was to be expected. There is nothing surprising in it. It is part of the democratic progress – an unhappy part. But unless we hate social progress wholesale we must be prepared for some evil results. That progress is real. It is true that the servant girl in the nineteenth century had a respect for books and culture when she was confronted with them, and that the servant girl of today (if she can be said to exist at all) has no respect for books or culture if by chance she is confronted with them. But the latter is much better off than the virtual slave who preceded her. There has been a revolution (it's absurd to think you can't revolve without blood) and already so much socialism has been attained that the really educated man is in a less favourable position than the emancipated slave. Whether this is good or bad depends upon one's humanitarian ideals and cultural ideals. But the light in which we regard it is not all-important. The fact that it is so with its concomitant cultural crisis calls for our chief attention. And the question which the outsider naturally asks is: What do the English intelligentsia do about it?

They do nothing.

That is surprising. For what one would expect them to do is so obvious. Here we have a race with a special flair for spontaneous organization. The richness of their capacity for doing this remains the envy of all other nations. The English love a crisis, for then their talent for organizing themselves is stimulated. When there is no big crisis on they content themselves with the promotion of innumerable Societies for the Furtherance, the Protection, or the Prevention of every possible activity. They prefer this to State assistance. Hospitals, schools and other organizations which elsewhere are run by the State are left to the people in England. They take a great pleasure in conscientiously running these societies. To be the Honourable Secretary of the Something Something is felt to convey an honour. The public spirit of many a lady thus engaged frequently makes up for her lack of private spirit. Most of these organizations are altruistic, charitable and ethical. One of them is aesthetic. The Society for the Protection of Rural Beauty is one of the most practically useful of all these activities, undoing with the right hand of the nation at least a quarter of the destruction wrought by the left hand. Thus external beauty receives a certain degree of attention and protection. But no protection is offered to the more subtle kinds of beauty belonging to culture.

This is strange. For it would seemingly be so easy. The idea would be to assist and protect, for instance, the philosophical-critical book of a vitalist and un-academic nature – work which published in the ordinary way would only sell five hundred copies. So a society or a club is formed called "The Intellectual Book of the Month Club." The subscriber would receive news each month of the best book (according to the Committee) and of others recommended – all these books being on a cultural level not likely to be bought by the public otherwise. In England there are said to be about forty-five million people. If one-forty-fifth of them, if a hundred thousand, if fifty thousand, if twenty-five thousand, if twelve thousand, if six thousand, if three thousand out of the forty-five million inhabitants of England (it is conceivable, though only just conceivable, that a few colonials from overseas might join in) paid a subscription to such a club so that a publisher could rely upon the sale of a thousand or more copies of a highbrow work – then English culture would be safe, and the intellectual leaders would be allowed to do their job and *lead*.

Such a nucleus is not to be found in England.

But there are plenty of similar clubs and societies. There is nothing unpractical about the club idea. All sorts of Book of the Month Clubs and Books of the Left and the Right Clubs carry on with great success each performing a useful office. While Crime Clubs and Murder Clubs get on grand. But there is no Intellectual Club. There is no demand that in the midst of the literary Vanity Fair there shall be set aside one booth in which the torch of Culture shall be proudly and firmly held aloft.

For this is England.

4

Thus we find ourselves facing the great difficulty about England for all who are not English. Here is a whole nation with an enormous population in which there is nowhere any passion for the absolute.

The English mind is an extraordinary thing. It fascinates the outsider by its lack of seriousness. An Englishman can be sincere – indeed he perspires with sincerity. He cannot be serious and consecutive. He has no desire to follow anything out to its ultimate conclusion (hence the powerful logic of Bertrand Russell has as much effect upon him as some "turn" in a music hall). He refuses to be fundamental. He cannot bear to reach an absolute belief about anything. He shirks taking *convictions* as final, though he will tolerate them no end as *views*. A convinced opinion enters one ear and makes a clean exit from the other changed into a "point of view." When this is impossible, when the convinced opinion before it can make a safe exit meets a completely opposing convinced opinion – he is not put out. He is not floored. He plays a trick: he says, with a certain lofty grandeur: "I suspect that the truth lies somewhere between these two extremes," and having said that he feels that not only has he been personally profound but that somehow the matter is disposed of and we can "steer our way" between the two convictions without running on any rocks. Very occasionally he enjoys the play of ideas and after a heated conversation will say: "Well, old man, I haven't agreed with a word you've said, but anyway we've had a jolly fine argument." When discussing some heart-breakingly vital issue he will suddenly flatten you out by saying: "Let's agree to differ." He will tell an author how much he has enjoyed his book, adding: "Not that I agree with all of it, you know. But that makes it all the more interesting, don't you think?" He used to say of Bernard Shaw: "I don't agree with him, of course; but he makes people *think*, and that's the main thing, isn't it?" By using the word agree or disagree he doesn't mean to imply that he himself has convictions, he simply means that he doesn't hold with anyone having convictions. By saying that he is *interested* he extracts the sting of passion from his opponent. It is a wonderful word for his purpose – interest. A debate, for instance, upon some knotty social problem, is broadcast by the BBC (the institution which reflects the best and worst qualities of England with the emphasis of an enlarged photograph). In the course of the debate someone makes a terse statement of convinced belief. You say to yourself: "By God, that's true!" But the moment he stops, the brilliantly competent conductor of the debate says with a sort of world-weary amiability: "That is a very interesting point of view." And the former statement immediately ceases to be a conviction, a truth, and is safely removed into the region of relativity.

Art, religion and philosophy (the ingredients of culture) move on the plane of passion and conviction. They do not belong to utilitarianism save in the ultimate sense that he who pursues such things may in the end prove a more desirable human being than the man who is satisfied with mental and spiritual garbage. But the intelligent Englishman, while not blind to such a consideration, really only wants "to get things done" and to arrive at some compromise between conflicting parties so that he can get in motion. His technique, as I have already pointed out when speaking of his qualities as a gentleman, is to be inoffensive at all costs and at all times. No one must be offended. This ideal is carried as far as it can very well go. If anyone is about to criticize somebody's work or business, the critique is preceded by: "He's a very nice man, indeed, but…" If some shocking evil or exploitation is in question, the speaker says: "I'm not accusing any particular person. It's not the person that is to blame but the system." If some bold fellow takes it upon himself to denounce something vigorously or to advance an unpopular view, he prefaces his remarks as follows: "What I am about to say must, I'm afraid, be unpalatable to many of you. It may cause deep offence. I know that many of those among my hearers, people for whom I have a sincere regard, hold a very different view. I do not wish to hurt anyone's feelings, but I beg you to believe that I cannot with a clear conscience..." He goes on like this for two or three minutes, after which time the audience or listeners-in are ready to forgive him – on the ground that "anyway he is absolutely sincere." I used to attend the meetings of a society which met once a month when one of the members read a paper. The papers varied in quality. But each paper was praised and spoken of as "the best" the club had so far heard. No point of view was ever taken seriously or thrashed out consequentially. No ass was ever made to feel that he was a quadruped. No vulgarian was ever made to feel embarrassed by the concealed embarrassment he caused others.

In this matter the English do really appear to reach an absolute. It is an absolute that everything must be made to go smoothly and to appear as innocuous as possible – hence conservatives so often agree to carry out in their name the socialistic reforms. The main thing is that no one must be disturbed in mind. The Senior Announcer at the BBC provides the best illustration of the English attitude here. An attitude is a question of *tone*. Tone over the air is everything. And power of tone is an English speciality. I have an unqualified admiration for that Announcer. In so far as any job can be done to perfection, there it is. It amounts to genius as much as any acting can, and sometimes – as on the Death of Kings – it approaches the sublime. He adopts the perfect tone for the disaster, the death, the news, the weather, the sports; this he does ideally, but his real powers are not called forth till he has to deal with some crisis or when something unEnglish is perpetrated – perhaps in the House of Commons. Then he is supreme. He *consoles* you. He can report some shocking blatancy, uttered by a public man who has forgotten to control himself, in such a soothing way as to remove all unpleasantness from it – even to make it a pleasantry. He can make a riot appear a street incident, a revolution an anticipated reform, a massacre a regrettable episode. This man, this consoler, is literally the Voice of England. In his tone is heard the accent of the national character. Amiability, gentility, good-natured appreciation of "all shades of opinion"; lack of rancour, hatred or malice; belief in the world-importance of England; and freedom from perturbation whatever is said or done – such are some of the qualities conveyed on the air by the tone of the Announcer.

All this makes for a high level of civilization. To find something to surpass it we would surely have to direct our gaze towards Ancient China.

5

It does not make for culture. So long as you can "give a speech to a mixed gathering without once offending the most delicate susceptibilities of any member of the audience," you are a gentleman. You cannot be an artist. The passionate belief, the unconventional thought, the original idea, the standard of excellence which must not be debased, can find no recognized place in the life of such a country. They are ruled out.

This atmosphere rules out the theatre save as a place of entertainment first and last. The *censorship* of the English theatre makes a curious comment upon English tolerance. We have noted above, everyone notes, the extent of that tolerance. It cannot be denied. The English take criticism of themselves, and criticize themselves, better than most nations – though, let me add, only very simple people think that the English do not mind damaging criticism – why should they not? They naturally do, and their method of dealing with it is to be silent on the main issue, to indulge in no violent justification or in an examination of the criticism, but to attack their opponent on irrelevant points, or say that he is *dull*; or that "though undoubtedly sincere, he is lacking in a sense of humour." That also is wisdom. And in some fields their intolerance might almost be called tyranny. It is not generally understood that the English theatre is spiritually, mentally and poetically starved owing to the astonishing stringency of the censorship. Yet such is the case. It is not lack of genius, but the refusal of genius, which has brought about the general state of affairs. People do not believe this because they cannot see the great works that have not been written – which would have been written. Take the case of Granville Barker – a potentially major dramatist, if ever. He was made to close down, to shut up shop, and devote himself to the safe and respectable study of Shakespeare – a cultural robbery, a cultural murder. Yet the extent of these crimes is only known to the progressive theatre managers – and what they have to tell of the censorship, its fantastic ruling in the name of sex or politics or religion (though chiefly of sex), would fill a volume of criminally funny stories. It is felt by the authorities that in view of the fact that the play is the most direct form of influencing people emotionally and mentally, the stage must not be allowed to say anything that could offend anyone, hurt anyone or stimulate anyone into unEnglish, mental, political or erotic activity. But the progressive theatre managers know that it is hopeless to plead with the intelligentsia for a revolution against the uneducated dictators who oppress them. For the intelligentsia could never be roused to *that* extent! They agree with the managers. They are extremely agreeable. On hearing his story they say: "We entirely agree with you. It is an incredible scandal. Yes indeed. Indeed yes." Clearly they wish it were otherwise. But they do not mind. They deplore the situation, but on the whole they prefer Mr Noel Coward. They realize that the creation of a great special theatre for good and advanced plays would solve the problem, but on the whole they feel it more important to support the hospitals. Riddled with utilitarianism and humanitarianism, they feel that the cultivation of the mind, the soul, the emotions is of small value compared with physical fitness.[1]

This atmosphere rules out a standard of literary excellence. No work can be great without style. But, allowing for the few really brilliant exceptions to this rule, style in England today means nothing, absolutely nothing to readers or critics. Worse, it is suspect. If anyone lets it be known that he really cares about style, the rumour goes round that he is an art-for-art's-sake man – beyond which there can be no greater condemnation. Yet every artist knows that what he says will not be effective unless he says it with style – his book will otherwise be a bungalow which will collapse soon after the owners have bought it. This obvious fact cuts no ice in England today. An enormous amount of books which can be read *once* with pleasure are published every week. As they do give that much pleasure they are legitimately praised. But the praise given employs phrases week after week which imply that these literary efforts are on the same level as imperishable works of literature. No doubt this sort of thing has happened in all ages and always will. But today no writer is ever in the least afraid that if he produces something intolerably cheap he may be made a public fool of in the papers. He knows that only once in a blue moon is space reserved for such a thing, and that in any case he is more likely to be praised. So much stronger is the commercial than the cultural pressure, that critical bumpings-off of literary gangsters and swindlers is out of the question.

Everything must be made to go along as smoothly as possible – for the sake of *commerce*. Hence it is thought best to abolish the dividing line between the commercial and the cultural. Thus the former can become the chief consideration in the field of literature, and the tendency to lay the emphasis elsewhere – as in the fields of medicine, priesthood and politics – can be quietly dropped. In so far as the cinema magnates speak of their Film Industry we must assume that we are back again in the factory. And though the term Literature Industry is not yet employed, it is clear from the advertisements, from certain books and from certain critics (I once thought one of them was selling shoes), that it exists. There is no reason why it should not exist. When the publishers of Mr Sydney Horler write up "Horler for Excitement" or others "Morly for Murder" we recognize that they have as much right to do so as other manufacturers have to write up "Bovril for Strength." To be an honest tradesman (if such an adjective may be permitted) is a sound thing to be. But no dividing line is set up between the Book Industry and Literature! The critics for the most part have thrown up the sponge. This suits the public – to whom the Standard of Excellence is identical with selling-power. He who answers this standard is admired more than any genius. In England a successful man is adored – nothing more is asked of him. (In Ireland the successful man is loathed and immediately becomes the Aunt Sally for malignant attack.) This runs very deep. It is amazing to note how some scandalous cheapener and letter-down of honest literary standards is promptly forgiven because he has made a pile of money out of it. There is a publicist writing today whose work has proved itself to be beyond even caricature, but quite intelligent people think it all right because of his sales. "Yes, but look at the *money* he makes out of it!" they say, their eyes moistening with greed. In England such writers are not regarded as the mortal enemies of culture.

This atmosphere rules out religion. Or rather, this atmosphere means that religion simply isn't there. The people are fundamentally irreligious. In place of religion they have ethics – good conduct, morality. So true is this that I think an English reader will hardly know what I mean. Religion is a question of poetry in the soul, of passion for the absolute, of rhythm in the heart, of feeling for the mystery, of love. This may not be goodness, but I believe it has some relation to a fundamental goodness in the heart. It is not cold morality from the head. And religion is one of the essentials of culture. It is lacking in England today. The reading of the Bible used to help a great deal and had a decisive influence upon English Literature. Now that the Bible is no longer read we see the negative result in the current literature – so lacking in poetry of the soul, in rhetoric, in swing, in flow, in drive, in melody, in mystery, in verve! No journal dares publish an article which contains these qualities. The Irish, with all their many faults, are a religious people, and when they find themselves up against this lack of soul-culture in the English they are inclined to become bewildered and abusive like Sean O'Casey when confronted by Mr James Agate or Mr Noel Coward.

Some may think it open to question whether this irreligiousness is fundamental. I can only say that I advance a conviction here rather than a prejudice. When a thing is true, it is chalked up everywhere. We cannot avoid condemning ourselves out of our own mouths. We see this irreligiousness mirrored by the various representatives of the people. Their Press is strictly *soulless* now. Not that religion, as they understand it, is excluded. Far from it. It is found to be quite a commercial asset. The response to religiosity is very considerable. There's money in it. The bigger papers find it a good thing to hire a religious expert. And what – to underline my chief point again – is their definition of religion? It is defined as "good activity." At the beginning of 1937 the *News Chronicle* published a series of New Year Wishes by experts concerning all sorts of subjects – Sport, Air, Foreign Policy, Theatre, etc. Mr Hugh Redwood, the religious expert, supplied the following wishes for religion: "A people's peace conference. A church militant, no longer content with rearguard actions. Greater charity born of greater compassion. Abolition of flag-days and a wide extension of personal service. Bolder adventures in housing, and less dragooning of council tenants. Temperance advertising with the same wit and humour as the liquor trade. The gift (for myself) of a road sense. Likewise of a car. Penny postage, and more people trying to say what they want in not more than a hundred words."

The attitude of the journalists towards religion compares favourably, however, with the attitude of those other representatives of the people – the politicians. Augustine Birrell – one of those exceedingly rare men who, never seeking greatness, have greatness thrust upon them – declared that in all his life he had never known a more irreligious atmosphere than that of the House of Commons. A few sniffs of it today make one feel pretty certain that it has not much changed since he wrote concerning Bradlaugh's condemnation: "Of all evils from which the lovers of religion do well to pray that their faith may be delivered, the worst is that it should ever come to be discussed across the floor of the House of Commons. The self-selected champions of the Christian faith who then ride into the lists are of a kind well calculated to make piety hide her head for very shame. Rowdy noblemen, intemperate country gentlemen, sterile lawyers, cynical but wealthy sceptics who maintain religion as another fence round their property, hereditary Nonconformists whose God is respectability and whose goal a baronetcy, contrive, with a score or two of bigots thrown in, to make a carnival of folly, a veritable devil's dance of blasphemy. The debates on Bradlaugh's oath-taking extended over six years and will make melancholy reading for posterity."

White-robed posterity! adorable abstraction of the human mind, so noble and just. But we are always reaching posterity; and it is doubtful whether a similar occasion today would provide a less melancholy spectacle.

And when the heavy and the weary weight of an English Sunday falls upon the streets, like silent thunder, how often one longs to go to a church and listen to the incomparable music of the prayers. What the prayers

An Irishman's England

actually and fact-ually say is not important, and yet they can convey the Spirit of the Divine into our hearts if pronounced rightly by a man of God. And how are they said by the clergyman in church? We know. We know how they are said, and we enter not in. They are not uttered by religious men. When they are so uttered, when their meaning and their mystery are given to us by a great orator and poet of God like Daniel Lamont, Moderator of the Church of Scotland, whose never-to-be-forgotten utterance was heard by the whole world at the Memorial Service to the death of George V, *then* we draw close to the core of religion. And how often, in England, do we hear the like of that?

It is therefore not surprising that as the people do not care for religion itself and prefer to take morality into their own hands, the Church of England is found less satisfactory than more progressive movements like Buchmanism which has taken the sensible course of frankly eliminating the elements of intelligence and spirituality. But in view of the fact that any literature not bearing sympathetically upon Groupism is proscribed by the members, we have to recognize yet another obstacle to the culture of this highly civilized nation.

We must agree, I think that in England morality and legality are considered to be *enough*.

In London there are many Temples. They are lovely and sequestered places. In the courts and around the arches there still lingers the cloistered atmosphere of a religious day that is done. Now no priest enters those gates. From those porches no Father descends. Through those corridors no faint echo of a prayer is heard. The empty gardens and the gracious lawns are closed against the poet and the scribe. And all, all is given over – to the Law.

6

The demand for what I venture to call culture is therefore not great. But instead there is a great demand for and a constant supply of first-class entertainment, the ingredients of which are sentimentality, cynicism, irony and humour. The overpowering sentimentality of the English is, of course, world-famous. It washes out the theory that they are unemotional, and establishes the direction into which their controlled emotionalism is channelled. And so long as sentimentality is somewhere in the background, cynicism is more popular than in any other country in the world (can you think of an exception?), because it is *the* irreligious quality.[2] There is a great response to irony in all classes, for the ironic phrase is the best soother of passionate protest: "the irony of it!" an Englishman will say, confronted by some massive piece of poetic injustice, and will dismiss it as an inherent principle of the universe – and this, again, is wisdom. But humour, pure and simple, is the exemplary English quality.

An Englishman cannot bear being told that he has no sense of humour (though he doesn't mind if he is accused of having no sense of wit). When describing his discomfitures he will say: "Luckily I'm so constituted that on such occasions I can't help seeing the humour of the situation, and I burst out laughing." And this also is wisdom – in the art of living without angry scenes.

Humour is *perspective*. One of the highest faculties of the mind. Vision of the whole. Instead of the event alone being seen, it is seen in relation to all other events surrounding it. Seeing this, we smile. We see the funny side no less than the tragic or exasperating side. If a man really lacks the sensation of humour he sees the world as a tragedy and his own life as a tragedy and the lives of others as tragedies. (There is a distinguished English critic now writing who really does possess no sense of humour – with the result that Tragedy is his only theme, and he cannot bear to write about anyone who was not a great hand at suffering.)

So far so good. But in the Englishman's hands humour is not always perspective. Not by a long chalk. It is often a shield against seriousness[3] and against profundity. At one time I had the honour to give a few lectures to an Adult Education Class consisting of some forty students at Morley College. In this class there was a Cockney of extremely lively intelligence who wrote and published books while carrying on with his trade as a carpenter. A sensitive man underneath. But incapable of seriousness. And "a born humorist." At the end of a lecture in these Adult Education classes there is a "discussion time." The Authorities regard "these discussions as the important thing." May I pause here for a second to note how very English that is? "The Discussion is the Chief Thing" – that is the guiding phrase of the educationalists who run this movement. But they've never thought it out, for in England one simply doesn't think anything out – never! – and an assumption once made and formulated is taken for granted for all time. It is conceivable that a lecturer might be capable of putting a pregnant thought or two before his class, thoughts which would need some digestion and which could perhaps profitably be brought up next meeting after the students had had time to think. Whereas an immediate discussion means that a wad of words and questions, mostly thoughtless and irrelevant, are stuck between the lecture and the students. But this could never be a consideration in England where a discussion of any kind, no matter how frivolous, is preferable to taking anything seriously... However to return, this man I was speaking of, this Cockney author, at the end of each lecture I gave, immediately used to rise to his feet and pour out a little flood of humorous commentary suggested by this, that or the other point in my lecture. It was remarkable. For as he spoke I saw each particular thing which I had said in my lecture being humorously disposed of, lifted clean out and safely removed from further serious consideration. An example? Rather difficult to give on paper; but supposing I spoke about the miraculous way we find ourselves acquiring tastes as we become more mentally alert and developed, an appreciation of music or poetry or painting which has lain dormant in us, etc. Here would be a "point" which my man would get hold of. "Mr Collis has spoken about acquiring tastes," he would begin, "I wish he would tell me how I can acquire a taste for tomatoes!" Laughter. Point disposed of. Likewise with all points of a fundamentally important nature. To follow them up, to work them out, really to believe them, might be awkward and would certainly be a nuisance.

Hence it is an enormous advantage in England for a philosopher to be "funny." If he does not possess the happy phrase he is in danger of being instantly and thoughtlessly dismissed as a person who "takes himself too seriously" or "is lacking in a sense of humour." In England a thing has to be considered pretty bad before it is "beyond a joke." Well, personally I think that the criticism in England of works which are above critics' heads, can only be described as beyond a joke. Until their man is dead they refuse to admit the superiority and to let the public sample the work. There are always exceptions, but for the most part the flippant, ironical, humorous attitude adopted towards any new and vital thinker is odious. There is no tradition that criticism should be affirmative, that it should take pride in telling the public what an important writer's contribution is. In England there is real pride and pleasure taken in pointing out what his contribution is *not*. There is no critical conscience. (But not for one moment do I pretend that the Irish are any better in this matter! It is necessary to look to France and to France alone for such a tradition.)

We must admit that the combination of humour and sentimentality, of the smile and the tear, has generated fine things from time to time. Only England could have produced a Dickens. Only England could have produced a Chaplin. The latter no less than the former reaches supremacy; yet I could not help being struck in *Modern Times* by one caption which seemed to me amazingly English in the circumstances. "I will make my living," says Charlie to the girl, "*even if I have to work for it.*" And everyone laughs. But this is the age of unemployment, and this particular picture shows crowds of unemployed, including Charlie, trying to get jobs. To stick in a remark so completely out of tune with the theme of modern times, struck me as strange. But no one minded in England, for it raised a laugh and glossed over the essential tragedy of unemployment.

No people are so good as the English at turning on the tap of humour when the occasion demands it. But the outsider would hurriedly emphasize what seems to him incontestable, namely that except when their comedians are men of genius their comedies are atrocious. It seems to me that an English comedy, as a piece of entertainment, is no laughing matter – whether in film or play or story or music hall. Perhaps the music hall provides the most striking example of the unfunny being greeted with prolonged laughter. It is possible for the outsider to sit through an entire evening's performance in the midst of a rocking audience without for one instant feeling inclined as much as to smile. Occasionally a man does come on who is funny, but this only makes it the more curious, for he gets neither more nor less applause than the next man. (Perhaps all the laughter is purely escapist?) Apart from its unfunniness the English music hall is intolerably vulgar – but maybe that is only because of the elimination of wit. What one might call the British pyjama joke provides the stranger with a really colossal lack of pleasure. But then the attitude to sex in England, from the suggestive, knowing giggle of the university man to the pyjama joke man, would demand a chapter to itself.

The reading public in England is a very large one (in Ireland it does not reach three figures), and it is satisfied with the work that can be produced from this synthesis of sentiment and humour. Biography, autobiography and fiction meet the demand. What is asked for in a book is character and story. To an Englishman it is self-evident – he is an amazing fellow at assumptions – that character and story are all anyone could ask for, and that thought and style and meaning and artistry are utterly unnecessary. His indifference to the fresh idea is famous. But I confess I cannot understand it! I cannot understand the lack of response to originality – without which quality an author doesn't count. The angle, the slant of a writer is surely the decisive criterion as to whether he ought to be on the job or not. But in England it counts against him! So long as he has character and story the clichéd thought, the clichéd phrase, the clichéd feeling are actually preferred to originality: and that is what I cannot understand – that the dull thing should *attract* more than the shining thing.

Further, if character and story are subordinated to landscape, then we find that the English "love for the countryside" is a pretty hollow thing. In his book on England, Wilhelm Dibelius observes with much penetration that "A great landscape artist like Turner had to wait long for recognition because he did not give the average Englishman the two things he understands in painting – portraits and anecdotes." Strikingly true! And still truer for the Turners of the pen. If Hardy had not known how to run his melodramatic plots he would never have been heard of, he would be simply a "prodigious bore" as that distinguished writer, Richard Aldington, calls him. The real greatness of Wordsworth to this day and to all eternity in England is and shall be underestimated, while the critics fasten their John Bulldog teeth into his character and affairs. What use have they for a Herman Melville, the man who sat and sits and shall for ever shine as a Shakespeare of the sea? Drive away anyone with a genius of his own which doesn't do exactly what all others do, make him tell a straight story or starve – that is the absolute decree in England upon the descriptive artist who is in any case rarer than any other. Tell a story, and we'll let you work in your stuff if you must. And so they starve or are cast out or struggle up like H W Tomlinson with some sort of a yarn.

I am not suggesting in these notes which I have the privilege to be writing concerning the educated people of England that they are any less "brainy" than other people. Quite the contrary. And we must admit that they are always looking round for means to exercise their highly developed faculties. Hence one finds in the papers all sorts of weekend competitions calling for a considerable degree of brain-power which it is felt can be more profitably spent in this manner than in reading one or more of such authors as were mentioned above by Davidson. And in view of the fact that odd bits of information become more and more highly thought of the further we recede from culture, a vogue for what are called cross-word puzzles has become a very popular way of passing the time amongst the intelligentsia and the unintelligentsia. One day, going into Mudie's Library, I found myself confronted with a whole table devoted to the display of books on how to do these puzzles. A whole table. Next to them in popularity, perhaps prior to them, come the detective stories which are turned out in the Crime Factory by skilled mental mechanics, and devoured between meals. But it would be unfair to suggest that this intellectual food completely exhausts the nourishment approved by the more refined palates; there is undoubtedly a distinct taste for verse provided it is written in blank prose and affords the reader an opportunity to display his cleverness in tracking down the meaning, hidden somewhere in the piece, like a corpse in a wood.

7

Granting, then, that the general public and the general intelligentsia feel no desire to organize a nucleus by which the torch of culture – so magnificently contributed to by the great English artists and prophets of all ages – may be kept alight, alive and influential, might one not look to the universities for assistance? To put such a question would be to mistake the nature of those institutions. Their purpose is utilitarian and social, not cultural. Students attend them in order to obtain degrees and hence a job, and to gain by the social atmosphere. To have been up at Oxford or Cambridge is regarded as "a great social asset." They have not been to a university, they have been to "the Varsity." Culture they may have, but that will be incidental, and not what is looked for. They could hardly be expected to do much clubbing together on a spiritual basis. It is equally out of the question that the dons should be invited to take a lead in this matter. They are cut off from partaking in the cultural life of the nation as conclusively as if they lived in Buckingham Palace. It is instinctively felt that they are "out of touch" and they are dismissed as "academic." So even if they did do something it might not have much effect. They can take part in the world's affairs with effect only if the professor part is somehow sunk. The English people do not look to professors for other than scientific light, if light that is. No modern Erasmus could reside at Oxford. It is not a cultural *centre* of the nation. The professors feel this themselves, and they shut the door, the world forgetting and by the world forgot. It is therefore with a certain unsmiling serenity that ex-university men who have added something to the reason, the light, or the beauty of the world, accept the cold-shouldering which is their portion if they communicate with their former professors.

How about the literary élite? Surely one might expect that the first move should be made by them?

At this point the reflections of a friendly observer of so great a country become still gloomier. The literary men could have saved the situation if they had wanted to. To make it clear again exactly what I mean: in the nineteenth century a book such as Newman's *Apologia Pro Vita Sua* was certain of an immediate reception and influence amongst a large body of co-operating élite. Today this élite, though still existing of course, has *allowed* the great flood of well-paid mediocrity to capture most of the publicity and sales: today such a book would not sell, while some fake pietist (however unconsciously so) sold edition after edition of his fake uplift. The modern élite have not looked after their own interests, they have betrayed their trust.

There is an Author's Club and an Author's Society. But when the members meet they talk exclusively upon one subject – their royalties and their sales. They get to know each other not with the purpose of exchanging views but with the hope that they may exchange reviews. That is as far as they get in cultural organization. Hence every young literary man is told that he hasn't a hope of getting on "unless he goes out to lunch and meets people." That is sound and human advice, but it is equivalent to saying that a writer's geographical position and strength of purse are the most valuable tools in his equipment.

However, it could not seriously be supposed that an Author's Club, necessarily composed of a heterogeneous number of writers, could co-operate in this way; but it might be supposed that some such spirit would be discernible amongst the élite. It is not discernible.

The outside student of England receives his impressions and formulates his conclusions. I have ventured to suggest that activity and utilitarianism presided over by morality and an ever-straining idealism may be said to differentiate the Englishman from others. But I would be either a very superficial, or inobservant, or timorous reporter if I did not add my signature to the old "nation of shopkeepers" assertion. That certainly is my finding also. I have often wondered whether really anything was more fundamental to the Englishman than commerce. In the commercial field itself, he is, as all the world knows, unsurpassed. He knows how to make things for sale, how to sell them and how to make people buy them. Even in unconscious ways he is wise to this end – hence you won't find a clock in Oxford Street, nor a clock in any big stores in London, for while people are buying things they must not be reminded of the time. The English businessman's emphasis on money has come in for plenty of satire from the hands of English literary men: "As is well known to the wise in their generation, traffic in Shares is the one thing to have to do with in this world. Have no antecedents, no established character, no cultivation, no ideas, no manners; have Shares." But even when we move outside the actual commercial field we discover that money is still the first consideration. I have frequently been amazed to find the extent to which sales count in the estimation in which an author is held even amongst the élite. The goodness of a sneered-at man's sales do really in the scoffers' own eyes make up for the badness of the work. (I know a man who wanted to call his book "Modern Prophets," but he had to change the title because whenever he mentioned it to his literary friends they all thought he meant *profits*.) Integrity – a much-used and popular word for some reason – easily snaps under the weight of the guiding principle of greed. Instead of creating a fortress against the philistines and existing independently of their approval, they support them in every way, flatter them and are paid by them. This is better than forming a Cultural Front – for you may "make a lot of money out of it," and the first question you will be asked, "howmuchdidyougetforthat?", can be answered with pleasure. One hears a lot of talk about cliques. But they scarcely exist. Isolation is the norm. It is easy to find two good poets living almost in the same street in Chelsea who neither know each other nor read each other – so busy are they trying to give the public what it wants.

But waiving the neglect of a Cultural Front, as something easier said than done, I am free to acknowledge that "things being as they are" in England, one cannot blame the attitude towards money of the literary man. For to be cultivated and poor in England eventually becomes intolerable. Though, it should be added with emphasis, this is truer in the country than in the town. Bernard Shaw said that every man over forty is a scoundrel. What he meant, I think, was that anyone living in England for as long as forty years necessarily becomes a brigand at heart, drops integrity ideals, compromises with the hard fact and fights the world with the old weapons of cunning and falsehood, saying: "Thou shalt die ere I die!"

However we look at it, we must acknowledge that the commercial spirit in this country, if not the ultimately decisive one, cuts very deep. D H Lawrence tells how the German philosopher, Count Keyserling, wanted to read *The Plumed Serpent*; for there is a great deal in common intellectually between that distinguished philosopher and that distinguished artist. "He tried to borrow a copy!" said Lawrence furiously. "He refused to buy one, the swine!" Perhaps furiously is wrong; but as humour it is weak.

8

Thus in England today the only man who receives no support from any quarter is the bearer of the purely cultural values. If he cannot support himself by some other means, or by pleasing the people instead of leading them, he is told that he must starve. In the summer of 1936 Bernard Shaw told me that he knew of "dozens of men of genius who are starving." He added: "Of course they really ought to pay to be allowed to live at all," which is an Irish way of stating the fact that an artist is really made to feel in England that it is awfully good of people to let him exist and not have him locked up or shot as an undesirable. And we may be sure that (in strong contrast with Russia) if ever the proletariat has a revolution in England, the artist will be still worse off – of that we may be certain. For the proletarians of England have been taught to believe that they are more important than the bearers of culture. They are taught to believe this by the intellectuals. Culture does not matter, they hear it said – no Left-Wing Nucleus is necessary to help it – but what does matter is the salvation of the proletariat. (As if these were antagonistic claims!)

This is one of the most interesting things about modern England – the ill-feeling towards those literary men who leave politics on one side. Propaganda for the keeping alive of spiritual values is dismissed, and the word propaganda severely reserved for work which impinges in some manner – no matter how feebly or uselessly – upon the political situation.[4] Art-religion-philosophy (an inseparable trinity when genuine) is regarded as an extra to be enjoyed provided that no Rome is burning. But as Rome is burning this must now be dropped altogether until the flames have been put out. The economic situation is too desperate to allow time for such a thing as art-philosophy-religion… A somewhat *thoughtless* attitude – since in this immensely complex world it seems unlikely that the material could be so conclusively divorced from the immaterial. The further point is also overlooked that the economic situation is actually less desperate than it used to be, while the psychic situation is much worse. The burning of the City of Culture might seem as worthy of a fire-brigade as the burning of the Political Situation.

It is natural that those who are engaged in putting out the flames of the latter should be ill-equipped for putting out the flames of the former, and vice versa – though there ought to be many who can do both. The strange thing is that only one of these Romes is considered to be burning, that only one fire-brigade is considered to be necessary. But no doubt many of those who feel that they should be political first and foremost and all the time, are probably personally wise since they never in any case could do much for the preservation of religious vision and true art and compassion and love; and as they are naturally more appreciated by the public they can and do boycott and cast contumely upon the lonely men who know that they have only one job and would be no good at political analysis however much they sacrificed their time and talents.

But let me close this aspect with a phrase that embraces the subject with a minimum of offensiveness. England is a country in which the social conscience is stronger than the artistic conscience.

Thus we return to the acknowledgement that though culture may be lacking, a high degree of civilization is achieved.

9

"Father MacAteer praised the Press representatives, saying their purpose had been an endeavour, which had been highly successful, to give their readers straightforward, simple facts, and yet the striking, pathetic stories were hallmarked with the gold stamp of their own glowing admiration for the frequently despised migratory labourers – heroes and heroines. For their efforts and those of their editorial chiefs he asked the people to join with him in rendering in the three-thousand-year-old language of the Gael a hundred thousand blessings of the God of Glory on their heads."

Thus was the Irish popular Press praised after the sea disaster at Aranmore Island when a boat-load of nineteen sank, and all save one were lost – ten of the bodies being unrecovered.

It is difficult to imagine such a tribute being paid at any time to the English popular Press. English reporters would not have regarded the affair as a tragedy. They would have regarded it as a "scoop."

Coming as I do from a country where the amount of words written down is very small, I can never pass by a Smith's book-stall without amazement at the quantity and variety of the magazines and newspapers placed at the people's disposal. It might be thought that one popular daily paper would be enough for the populace, that there could not be room for four or five. There is room. The same people never take two papers. For this, as I have said above, is the country of *classes*. Nothing witnesses to this fact so eloquently as the papers: a different class, a different type of person is catered for by each – not just a question of political views, for if and when the people have views on politics they do not take them seriously from the papers. But it is most interesting to note the different shades of intelligence called for by each. So marked is this that one knows at sight whether a given person would take in a given paper. The editors seem to know exactly what their respective readers will stand for in the way of advertisements. Thus perhaps only one of them would go so far as to publish a page devoted to a sketch and explanation of how the Inferiority Complex can be eradicated – the sketch showing a head divided into various Zones of Intelligence, Will, Ambition, Fear, Love and so on. These papers, by their pictures, advertisements, and news-stories mirror with glass-like purity the mind of the man in the street, now more educated than he used to be. With the exception of a few thrillers they supply the only literature which is read by millions of this famously individual nation. This is a new fact in the history of England. The radio, the newspaper and the cinema have closed the local libraries in many places.

These popular papers are often extremely interesting and entertaining. A large portion of the intelligentsia support now one now the other, and of course are delighted to write for them if they get a chance. Recognizing the existence of this public the editors generally arrange to hire some clever man to run a column in which he satirizes the values intrinsic to most of the paper. This is the soundest possible policy in view of the English love of humour before seriousness or integrity. One of these humorists – a clever man always careful to laugh at what is highbrow as well as at what is lowbrow – is now as popular amongst the intelligentsia as Mickey Mouse. The gentlemanly virtues of delicacy, restraint of emotion and respect towards it, sincerity, charity, lack of inquisitiveness, are waived for the sake of readers. Yet supposing one visits some of the people who run these papers, one finds that they are practically all gentlemen. They possess in themselves the above qualities – but they don't like to disappoint the mob. They are all gentlemanly idealists – and yet commercialism has them by the throat!

Sincerity is the hall-mark of the English people. They scent insincerity almost as if they had an extra sense. Hence Press campaigns often have no influence at all. For the readers cannot be persuaded about something by anyone if they are not sure that he is sincere – and they turn away more often than is realized from cynical sentimentality and from insincere sincerity.

Sometimes one would think that the popular Press is especially designed to prevent the new barbarians from ever being able to *read* (which is also an art). The essence of literary format lies in *the paragraph*. By merely turning over the pages of a book and observing the lie of the paragraphs, the skilled critic can tell instantly whether the author knows how to write or not. If an author cannot shape his paragraphs it means that he cannot shape his thought, his material, cannot give it to the reader whole. If he does not understand this and grasp its connection with that other essential in literature, *pace*, he must inevitably fail to produce the genuine article.

He can produce the newspaper article. It is instructive to note what is required of the writer of popular journalism in England. The various Schools of Journalism teach their pupils to use a new paragraph for every statement or face (not idea, for ideas are now ruled out unless they can be dressed as facts or morals). And very necessary teaching it is, for no article can be accepted if it is not written in these short paragraphs regardless of whether the writer gives anything whole to the reader. A journalistic paragraph can only be passed as such if it is not longer than five lines – hence if a certain statement or array of facts cannot be made in four to six lines, a new paragraph must be started up and the train of thought clipped in two. This kind of thing is more injurious to the untutored eye than any amount of slang could ever be. It militates against the reader's possible appreciation of literature – by which I do not mean a kind of frigid perfectionism, but the living word. It prepares the ground for the host of writers who sin against that word on every page they write.

Thus it may happen that the English language, as literature, will soon perish altogether. That would be a pity. Though the English are justly accused of claiming that they possess the best of everything, all nations agree to do homage to the power of the English tongue. It is so resourceful that a De Quincey or a Bertrand Russell find it equally serviceable. If a writer finds it convenient to employ two or three different styles, this instrument affords him the opportunity, allowing an exhaustive range from poetic perspective to the logic of wit, from lofty consideration to colloquial eloquence.

However, an Irishman cannot speak of the English language with the detachment of a foreigner. For we have not found it difficult to express the Irish spirit through those rhythms. I have quoted above the words spoken by a priest at the graveside of the victims at Aranmore. They are translated from the Gaelic. During his speech he also said that his hearers "would, especially during this month of the Holy Souls, pray earnestly for the repose of the souls of those who had gone from them. They would join in spirit with him, looking towards the coffins and the sea which, until God ordained otherwise, must serve as a shroud for the ten imprisoned dead, when he said: 'May angels conduct thee to Paradise. May the martyrs take charge of thy approach and lead thee into the Holy City of Jerusalem amidst the angelic chorus, and with Lazarus, at one time a poor man, may thou have rest eternal.'"

Such words witness to the beauty and fervour of the Gaelic language: but their translation into the English has not injured that fervour – owing to the Authorised Version of the Bible. Hence many Irishmen have felt drawn to the English tongue, and in taking it across the sea have striven to keep alive within it the poetry of religious feeling for the expression of which it is so beautifully adapted.

It may be objected that during all the foregoing I have neglected to acknowledge the supreme place which English poetry occupies in the world's literature, witnessing to the real passion, depth, imagination and cultivation of soul that lies under the glacial, the sober, and the culturally barbarous exterior of the people. True. No one is a keener student or subscribes more heartily than I do to that achievement. The fact that the world's greatest poet and dramatist is English must make us pause. And it is certainly very satisfactory for the English to have such artists, for then however badly they may treat them, the fact of their existence makes it impossible for unpalatable generalizations to be made about themselves! But does the splendour of English poets necessarily reflect the people? Might they not be eccentrics, representative of what the people *lack* rather than what they are, *au fond*? The actual existence of the giants is no problem, and their supremacy is, I think, best explained by Salvador de Madariaga when he says that the secret of England's possessing the greatest poets is that when her geniuses can be purely passionate they are also "born of the people of action endowed with a rich substratum of moral values. And it is obvious that such a combination is the ideal one for the creation of great art."

When contradictions are also combinations they undoubtedly bear the richest fruit. And it is true that in England the contradiction seldom fails to be a combination. Nevertheless whatever slick psychological theory we adopt (you can buy them seven for sixpence) to square the problem, we are bound to face the fact that the people of England almost to a man are moral and utilitarian, and they really only respond to these elements in their writers (consider the literature of commentary upon Wordsworth or Shelley or Byron!). And it seems to me quite as sound to listen to the critics as to the poets in order to hear the voice of England.

Finally, I cannot be persuaded that the English people as a whole love the object in front of them – which is the essence of all art and poetry in the soul. Recently Broadstone Station in Dublin closed down for ever. On the evening of the last day all those connected with it came to say good-bye – the occasion being broadcast. It was an Irish leave-taking in every way. The station was seen in its own right as a wonderful place dedicated to the coming and to the going of men. The chief official, standing resolutely before the microphone, said: "Farewell, a long farewell to all thy greatness!" That was all. It was enough. In those words he saluted the mystery of life and paid homage to the poetry that belongs to a railway station no less than to the loftiest creations of God or Man.

That is not how an English official would have wound up similar proceedings. That is not the light in which he would have seen the station. Instead of apostrophizing Euston or Paddington, crying: "Farewell, a long farewell to all thy greatness!" he would have stood self-consciously before the microphone and said: "It is with much regret that all of us here connected with the LNWR take leave of Euston Station. I am very grateful for the many tributes which I have received from all quarters on behalf of those who have worked here for so long. I firmly believe that this station has rendered greater service to the community than any other during the last fifty years. Before taking my leave, I should like to thank…"

1 By the time these words are printed the fight against this inertia may have been won at last.
2 It is not impossible to reach a fairly comprehensive statement with regard to English taste here. Pure sentiment, behind which there is little humour and no suggestion of flippancy, cynicism or irreverence – such as Helen Thomas' *As It Was* – may result in a fine achievement. But the English react very badly to it – it is far too serious and wounding for them. Pure detachment from the sentimental, such as John Collier carried out in his brilliant *Defy the Foul Fiend*, is an achievement at the other end. But again such a book is too alarming for the English to relish.
3 My account in *The Sounding Cataract* of Maxton's reception at a meeting of the Fabian Society when he became cutting brings this out concretely.
4 On the other hand, I wish emphatically to disassociate myself from any kind of sneer at the expense of the genuine Left-wingers who do say something. I know nothing in modern literature superior to Auden's poem – "Spain." It is a dynamic masterpiece – capable, I should say, of unlimited influence upon the whole communist movement.

John Stewart Collis

Bound Upon a Course

Bound Upon a Course takes a generous glance at the life of the celebrated biographer, John Stewart Collis. In this autobiography, Collis recounts his difficult childhood in Ireland, his decision to write, the years spent on the cultural fringe in London, and his acquaintance with the literary personalities of Rose Macaulay, W B Yeats and T S Eliot. But it was his decision to work on the land in 1940, which marked a watershed in his career. These rural experiences shaped his philosophy and resulted in the undisputed classic *The Worm Forgives the Plough*. Subtle, modest and acutely perceptive, this is an intriguing portrait of a man who was a unique synthesis of scientist, scholar and poet.

Farewell to Argument

In this intriguing glimpse at East and West, John Stewart Collis sets out his case that the West should lead the world into a new spiritual age by moving beyond the bounds of industrialisation. In putting forward this argument he compares the contribution of Gandhi and D H Lawrence and finds Lawrence's thinking on the new spirituality to be more compelling. *Farewell to Argument* outlines the philosophy that led John Stewart Collis to be labelled a pioneer of the ecological movement.

JOHN STEWART COLLIS

MARRIAGE AND GENIUS

'Few of us know much about the married life of even our closest friends. Nothing is so secretly guarded as this matter.' With this thought, John Stewart Collis sets out to examine the specific roles played by the wives of Strindberg and Tolstoy.

For Strindberg, three times married, the failure of his principal relationships was a source of guilt and suffering. For Tolstoy, marriage to Sonya Behrs eventually brought disillusionment and conflict. Using his rare literary skill, John Stewart Collis interweaves intimate details and public facts of both men with compassion and insight.

SHAW

In this acclaimed study of fellow Irishman, George Bernard Shaw, Collis writes with characteristic subtlety and perception. He portrays this immensely important freethinker, playwright, campaigner and journalist whilst debunking the myth that Shaw was a shameless self-publicist. Collis does not shy away from less palatable aspects of Shaw's personality. In this short, critical account he paints a vivid picture of a man who fought valiantly for Humanity while often forgetting the human beings around him.

John Stewart Collis

The Vision of Glory

The Vision of Glory is a highly original examination of natural phenomena and of how all things are interconnected. Combining scientific accuracy with beautiful prose, it is also a splendid poetic study of man's relationship with his environment.

'John Stewart Collis' divine gift is to explain the extraordinary nature of the ordinary' – *The Sunday Times*

The Worm Forgives the Plough

The Worm Forgives the Plough combines two works of John Stewart Collis. The first, *While Following the Plough*, is a highly personal account of his experience as a labourer on the land during the Second World War. Written with intense personal feeling, this book defines John Stewart Collis' philosophy on nature and man's relationship to the land. The second, *Down to Earth*, is an extraordinary series of meditations on remarkably prosaic things, such as the potato, the plough, the ant and the dunghill. Collis is a unique combination of scientist and poet and in this remarkable book he shows his rare love and understanding of the world around him.

'He is the poet among modern ecologists' – *The Times*

OTHER TITLES BY JOHN STEWART COLLIS AVAILABLE DIRECT FROM HOUSE OF STRATUS

Quantity		£	$(US)	$(CAN)	€
	An Artist of Life: Havelock Ellis	8.99	14.99	22.50	15.00
	Bound Upon a Course	8.99	14.99	22.50	15.00
	The Carlyles	8.99	14.99	22.50	15.00
	Christopher Columbus	8.99	14.99	22.50	15.00
	Farewell to Argument	8.99	14.99	22.50	15.00
	Leo Tolstoy	8.99	14.99	22.50	15.00
	Living With a Stranger	8.99	14.99	22.50	15.00
	Marriage and Genius	8.99	14.99	22.50	15.00
	Shaw	8.99	14.99	22.50	15.00
	The Sounding Cataract	6.99	12.95	19.95	13.50
	The Vision of Glory	8.99	14.99	22.50	15.00
	The Worm Forgives the Plough	8.99	14.99	22.50	15.00

ALL HOUSE OF STRATUS BOOKS ARE AVAILABLE FROM GOOD BOOKSHOPS OR DIRECT FROM THE PUBLISHER:

Internet: www.houseofstratus.com including synopses and features.

Email: sales@houseofstratus.com please quote author, title and credit card details.

Order Line: UK: 0800 169 1780,
USA: 1 800 509 9942
INTERNATIONAL: +44 (0) 20 7494 6400 (UK)
or +01 212 218 7649
(please quote author, title, and credit card details.)

Send to:
House of Stratus Sales Department
24c Old Burlington Street
London
W1X 1RL
UK

House of Stratus Inc.
Suite 210
1270 Avenue of the Americas
New York • NY 10020
USA

PAYMENT

Please tick currency you wish to use:

☐ £ (Sterling)   ☐ $ (US)   ☐ $ (CAN)   ☐ € (Euros)

Allow for shipping costs charged per order plus an amount per book as set out in the tables below:

CURRENCY/DESTINATION

	£(Sterling)	$(US)	$(CAN)	€(Euros)
Cost per order				
UK	1.50	2.25	3.50	2.50
Europe	3.00	4.50	6.75	5.00
North America	3.00	3.50	5.25	5.00
Rest of World	3.00	4.50	6.75	5.00
Additional cost per book				
UK	0.50	0.75	1.15	0.85
Europe	1.00	1.50	2.25	1.70
North America	1.00	1.00	1.50	1.70
Rest of World	1.50	2.25	3.50	3.00

PLEASE SEND CHEQUE OR INTERNATIONAL MONEY ORDER.
payable to: STRATUS HOLDINGS plc or HOUSE OF STRATUS INC. or card payment as indicated

STERLING EXAMPLE

Cost of book(s):..................................... Example: 3 x books at £6.99 each: £20.97
Cost of order:....................................... Example: £1.50 (Delivery to UK address)
Additional cost per book:........................... Example: 3 x £0.50: £1.50
Order total including shipping:..................... Example: £23.97

VISA, MASTERCARD, SWITCH, AMEX:

☐☐☐☐ ☐☐☐☐ ☐☐☐☐ ☐☐☐☐

Issue number (Switch only):
☐☐☐

Start Date: Expiry Date:
☐☐ / ☐☐   ☐☐ / ☐☐

Signature: _____

NAME: _____

ADDRESS: _____

COUNTRY: _____

ZIP/POSTCODE: _____

Please allow 28 days for delivery. Despatch normally within 48 hours.

Prices subject to change without notice.
Please tick box if you do not wish to receive any additional information. ☐

House of Stratus publishes many other titles in this genre; please check our website
(**www.houseofstratus.com**) for more details.